CHINESE
Characters
in Pictures

（2）

汪 春 郑重庆 编著
曹伟业 插图绘画

华语教学出版社
SINOLINGUA

First Edition   2005
Fourth Printing 2016

ISBN 978-7-80200-102-2
Copyright 2005 by Sinolingua Co., Ltd
Published by Sinolingua Co., Ltd
24 Baiwanzhuang Road, Beijing 100037, China
Tel: (86) 10-68320585 68997826
Fax: (86) 10-68997826 68326333
http://www.sinolingua.com.cn
E-mail: hyjx@sinolingua.com.cn
Facebook: www.facebook.com/sinolingua
Printed by Beijing Jinghua Hucais Printing Co., Ltd

Printed in the People's Republic of China

Preface

The American poet Ezra Pound once said, "The easiest language in the world for writing poetry is Chinese." And in the words of E. E. Cummings, another American poet, "Chinese poets are painters." This book, *Chinese Characters in Pictures* is one which uses words to explain and pictures to illustrate the form and structure of Chinese characters. Therefore, it is both a collection of poetry and a picture album, so to speak.

Each Chinese character has a form of its own, representing a particular sound and a particular meaning, one at least. In other words, each character is a unity of form, sound and meaning. The student of Chinese must call on every one of the individuals if he or she is to really know the personality of each.

Learning Chinese is quite different from learning any other language. The way of learning is different. In learning a Western language, for instance, you swallow a whole series of sounds, lock, stock and barrel. If you were to take a word apart, separating it into so many phonetic syllables, it would lose its meaning altogether. In learning Chinese, however, what you have to do is exactly that, not into so many syllables, but into so many characters. You learn first the characters, then the word. Take, for instance, the Chinese word 大学 (dà xué) which means "university". You first learn the words 大 and 学 separately since 大学 is formed by combining the two characters (you might call them elements of language). In meaning, 大学 has to do with both 大 and 学, and yet 大学 is not a simple case of 大 plus 学. 大学 is the Chinese equivalent of the English word "university". But if you were to take the English word "university" and try to figure out its meaning based on the meanings of the five syllabic components u/ni/ver/si/ty, you would definitely get nowhere, because separately, these components have no meaning at all and certainly have nothing to do with what the word "university" means. So, the character forms the basis in learning Chinese, whereas the word or sentence forms the basis for learning a Western language. It is no wonder then that there should have been so many textbooks written since ancient times on learning Chinese characters, e.g. *Qian Zi Wen* (Learn A Thousand Characters) and *Bai Jia Xing* (One Hundred Family Names).

The pictures as represented in the Chinese characters vary in complexity. Take the characters contained in this book. Some are as simple as 人,口,牛,羊; others as complicated as 双, 养, 喜, 声. Whether simple or complicated, they are each a picture and a poem. Of course, one cannot expect everyone to agree in their analyses of each and every character, just as people couldn't totally agree, in fact they might totally disagree, in their understanding and interpretation of a painting or a poem. Regardless of whether the poet or painter agrees or disagrees, the reader or viewer would have his own appreciation of the work on the basis of his or her own understanding. The same holds true, more or less, for the written script. It is your right to create the written character, it is my right to interpret it.

Chinese Characters in Pictures is written for those non-Chinese who intend to explore the secrets of the civilization. It is somewhat like a guidebook, listing nearly two hundred cultural sites. Like the looking glass in *Alice in Wonderland,* the characters depicted in this book will take the tourist into the kaleidoscopic world that is Chinese culture.

by Cheng Xianghui
Dean of College of Chinese Language
University of Macao

前言

美国诗人埃兹拉·庞德曾经说过:"世界上最适合写诗的语言是汉语。"美国另一位诗人E.E.卡明斯说:"中国诗人都是画家。"《画说汉字》用语言诠释、用图画演示汉字的结构和字形,因此可以说:这本书既是诗集又是画册。

每个汉字都有其独特的字形、特别的发音和至少一个字义。换句话说,每个汉字都是字形、声音和意义的统一体。学习汉语的学生必须接触每一个汉字才能真正了解它们的个性。

学习汉语的方法不同于学习其他语言。例如在西方语言中,若干个毫无意义的音节构成一个词,如果你把一个词拆分成音节,它的意义就不复存在。但是学习汉语则不同,你要做的恰恰是把一个词拆分成独立的字,在学习词之前先要学习字。以汉语"大学"(university)为例,你先要分别学习"大"和"学"这两个字,因为"大学"这个词是由这两个字组成的(你可以称它们为"语素")。从词义上看,"大学"和"大"和"学"有关系,但并不等于"大"和"学"这两个字义的简单相加。和"大学"对应的英文是university,如果你试图通过这个英文单词的五个音节u/ni/ver/si/ty推断出它的意思,那将是白费力气,因为这些音节没有意义,和词义毫无关联。词或句子是西方语言的基本元素,而汉语的基本元素是汉字。正是因为如此,从古至今,学习汉字的书层出不穷,如:《千字文》,《百家姓》等。

用以表示汉字的图形繁简不一。拿这本书中涉及的字来说,有些非常简单,象"人"、"口"、"牛"、"羊",有些却非常复杂,象"双"、"养"、"喜"、"声"。不论简单还是复杂,每一个字都象是一幅画、一首诗。也许并非所有人都赞同本书中对每个汉字的诠释,就象每个人对诗歌或绘画都有不同的理解一样,不论原创者有着怎样的寓意,读者或观者总是会在欣赏时加入自己的理解,对汉字的理解也或多或少地符合这一规则。

《画说汉字》是为那些希望探究中国文明史的外国朋友编写的,它就象一本旅游手册,带领读者徜徉于近200个"文化名胜";书中的汉字就象《爱丽斯漫游奇境》中的魔镜,引导旅游者进入中国文化的万花筒。

程祥徽

澳门大学汉语学院院长

Contents

隘

ài

(mountain pass)

阝	阝	阝	阝	阝	阝	阝	阝	陷	陷	隘	隘

　　这是一个象形字。左边的"阝"是"阜"的简写，表示"高山"。右边的"益"意思是"附加"，表示"在山顶用土修建防御工事"。两部分和在一起指战略要地，或山的关口。

A pictogram. "阝" on the left is an abbreviation of 阜, meaning a tall mountain. The other half, 益, meaning addition, implies that an earthen defence is built on the top of a mountain. The combination means a place which is strategically located and difficult to access, or simply a mountain pass.

【部首】 Radical 　　　阝 (ear)

【同部首字】 Characters under the radical
　　阴(cloudy)，阻(block)，除(get rid of)

【词语】 Words and phrases

隘口	àikǒu	(mountain) pass
隘路	àilù	narrow passage
隘巷	àixiàng	a narrow lane; alley
狭隘	xiá ài	narrow-minded
要隘	yào ài	a strategic pass

心胸狭隘

　　xīn xiōng xiá ài

　　　narrow-minded; intolerant

狭隘的山道

　　xiá ài de shān dào

　　　mountain trail

【例句】Example

　　到那个村庄的最短路线不是那条主公路，而是一条狭窄的、簇叶丛生的隘路。

　　　dào nà ge cūn zhuāng de zuì duǎn lù xiàn bú shì nà tiáo zhǔ gōng lù, ér shì yì tiáo xiá

　　　zhǎi de, cù yè cóng shēng de ài lù

　　　　The shortest route to the village isn't by the main road but by a
　　　　narrow, overgrown track.

àn

(dark; hidden)

| 丨 | 刀 | 刀 | 日 | 日` | 日ʸ | 日ʸ | 日ʸ | 昣 | 晬 | 晻 | 暗 | 暗 |

　　这个字由两部分组成：左边的"日"字代表太阳，所以它与光线有关；右边的"音"则与发音有关。"暗"就是因为光线不足而引起的，于是就造出了这个"暗"字。

This pictophonetic character comprises two parts. On the left is the character 日 (sun), and on the right 音 (hidden, secret). The combination suggests darkness due to insufficient light.

【部首】 Radical 　　　日(sun)

【同部首字】 Characters under the radical
　　　明(bright)，晓(dawn)，旷(vast)

【词语】 Words and phrases

暗藏	àncáng	hide; conceal
暗娼	ànchāng	unlicensed (or unregistered) prostitute
暗淡	àndàn	dim; faint
暗害	ànhài	kill secretly; stab in the back
暗井	ànjǐng	blind shaft; winze
暗探	àntàn	secret agent; detective
暗笑	ànxiào	laugh in (or up) one's sleeve; snigger
暗语	ànyǔ	code word

暗无天日

    àn wú tiān rì

        complete darkness; total absence of justice

暗渡陈仓

    àn dù chén cāng

        do one thing under the cover of another; illicit activities

暗送秋波

    àn sòng qiū bō

        make eyes at sb. while others are not looking; make secret overtures to sb.

【例句】 Example

    他暗示要我走开。

        tā àn shì yào wǒ zǒu kāi

            He hinted that he wanted me to leave.

百

bǎi

(a hundred)

| 一 | 一 | 丆 | 丆 | 百 | 百 | 百 |

当我们比较白和百时，就会发现它们的发音相同：(bai)。原来，后者是由前者演变来的，本来它是指白色、明亮的意思。但有时文字的发展很奇怪，它后来竟渐渐发展成数目字，而"百"就是十的十倍了。

By comparing two ancient Chinese pictograms "△" and "△", both pronounced as bɑi, we find the latter is derived from the former, which means white or bright. How it came to mean a hundred is not clear.

【部首】Radical   白(white)

【同部首字】Characters under the radical
皂(black)，皆(all)，泉(spring of a small stream)

【词语】Words and phrases

百般	bǎibān	in a hundred and one ways; in every possible way; by every means
百倍	bǎibèi	a hundredfold; a hundred times
百部	bǎibù	the tuber of stemona (Stemona japonica or Stemona sessilifolia)
百合	bǎihé	lily
百货	bǎihuò	general merchandise

百年	bǎinián	a hundred years; a century
百万	bǎiwàn	million
百姓	bǎixìng	common people

百读不厌

bǎi dú bú yàn

be worth reading a hundred times

百感交集

bǎi gǎn jiāo jí

all sorts of fellings well up in one's heart

百孔千疮

bǎi kǒng qiān chuāng

riddled with gaping wounds; afflicted with all ills

百川归海

bǎi chuān guī hǎi

all rivers flow to the sea; all things tend in one direction

百思不解

bǎi sī bù jiě

remain puzzled after pondering over sth. a hundred times; remain perplexed despite much thought

百尺竿头，更进一步

bǎi chǐ gān tóu, gèng jìn yí bù

make still further progress

【例句】Example

这个故事百听不厌。

zhè gè gù shì bǎi tīng bú yàn

You never get tired of hearing this story.

北

běi

(north)

| 丨 | 十 | 丬 | 北 | 北 |

这是一个会意字。甲骨文中的"北"字是两个背靠背坐着的人。古人认为应该面向南而坐，如果向北而坐就是坐反了。

An ideogram. It derived from "𠤎" found on oracle bones depicting two persons sitting with their backs to each other. Ancient Chinese used to think that facing the south was the correct way of sitting, while facing the north was thought to be sitting backward.

【部首】Radical　　丨 (vertical line)

【同部首字】Characters under the radical
　　旧 (old)，出 (go out)，中 (center)

【词语】Words and phrases

败北	bàiběi	defeat
北斗星	běidǒuxīng	the Big Dipper; the Plough
北方	běifāng	north; the northern part of the country, esp.the area north of the Huanghe river; the North
北极	Běijí	the North Pole; the Arctic Pole; the north mangetic pole
北京	Běijīng	Beijing(Peking)
北美洲	Běiměizhōu	North America
北温带	běiwēndài	the north temperate zone

北伐战争

    běi fá zhàn zhēng

        the Northern Expedition(1926-1927)

北国风光

    běi guó fēng guāng

        northern scenery

北回归线

    běi huí guī xiàn

        the Tropic of Cancer

北洋军阀

    běi yáng jūn fá

        the Northern Warlords(1912-1927)

【例句】Example

    我生在南方，但从小生活在北方。

        wǒ shēng zài nán fāng, dàn cóng xiǎo shēng huó zài běi fāng

        I was born in the South, but I've settled in the North since my childhood.

贝

bèi

(cowrie; shellfish)

| 丨 | 冂 | 刀 | 贝 |

象形字里，"贝"（）的上面是外壳（），下面是触角（丨丨）。当我们取走壳里的生物后，剩下来的空壳便叫"贝"。以前的原始人早就懂得用贝壳来造装饰品，它曾经也被用作钱币呢！

A pictogram, 贝 refers to the empty shell which remains after the meat of the clam inside is removed. Its origin found on oracle bones looked like this " 貝 ". The upper part " 貝 " represents the shell and the lower part " 丨丨 " the clam's two feelers. From the artifacts unearthed by archaeologists, we discover that the primitive people were very fond of decorating themselves with stringed shells.

【部首】 Radical   贝(shell)

【同部首字】 Characters under the radical
贞(loyal)，贡(tribute)，财(wealth)

【词语】 Words and phrases

贝雕	bèidiāo	shell carving
贝壳	bèiké	shell
贝类	bèilèi	shellfish; molluscs
贝母	bèimǔ	the bulb of fritillary (fritillaria thunbergii)
贝丘	bèiqiū	shell mound

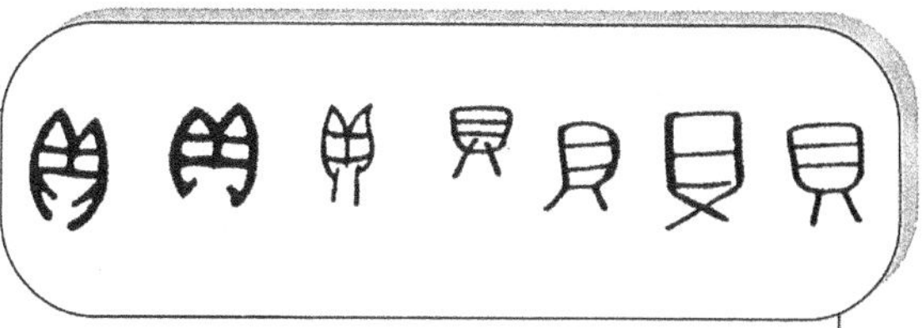

贝壳细工

bèi ké xì gōng

shell work

贝阙珠宫

bèi què zhū gōng

underwater palace decorated with shells and pearls; imperial palace

【例句】Example

孩子们在海中拾到许多贝壳。

hái zǐ mén zài hǎi zhōng shí dào xǔ duō bèi ké

The children picked up many sea shells at the seashore.

奔

bēn

(to run)

| 一 | 广 | 大 | 大 | 本 | 本 | 奔 | 奔 |

会意字。在金文中，"奔"（）的上半部（大）显示的是一个挥臂奔跑的人，下半部（止止）是三只脚，表示腿的快速运动。现在这个字形是从小篆演变而来的，所以字型有了很大变化。

Ideogram. In metal language* "大", the upper part "大" shows a man running with swaying arms and the lower part "止止", three feet, depicting the rapid movement of his legs. A clear sign that a man is running. The present form of the character was evolved from the Little Zhuan (script used during Qin Dynasty, 221-206 BC, and which appeared later than metal language). It is thus indistinguishable from its original form.

*metal language: scripts inscribed on bronzes found prior to Qin Dynasty.

【部首】 Radical　　大(big)

【同部首字】 Characters under the radical
夸（praise），夺（seize），奖（prize）

【词语】 Words and phrases

奔波	bēnbō	rush about; be busy running about
奔驰	bēnchí	run quickly; speed
奔跑	bēnpǎo	run
奔袭	bēnxí	long-range raid

| 奔泻 | bēnxiè | (of torrents) rush down; pour down |
| 奔走 | bēnzǒu | run; rush about; be busy running about |

奔走呼号

　　bēn zǒu hū háo

　　　go around campaigning for a cause

热情奔放

　　rè qíng bēn fàng

　　　overflowing with enthusiasm

四散奔逃

　　sì sàn bēn táo

　　　flee in all directions; flee helter-skelter; stampede

铁水奔流

　　tiě shuǐ bēn liú

　　　molten iron pouring out in a stream; racing current

长江之水，奔腾不息

　　cháng jiāng zhī shuǐ, bēn téng bù xī

　　　The mighty waters of the Yangtze River roll on incessantly.

奔走相告

　　bēn zǒu xiāng gào

　　　run around spreading the news; lose no time in telling each other the news

【例句】 Example

骏马在草原上奔驰。

　　jùn mǎ zài cǎo yuán shàng bēn chí

　　　Sturdy steeds gallop on the grasslands.

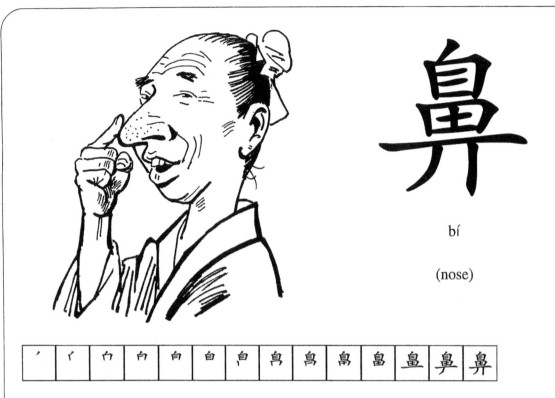

鼻

bí

(nose)

丿	亻	冂	白	白	自	自	臼	臼	鼻	畠	畠	鼻	鼻

　　这个字最初写做"自"，字形就像一个鼻子。后来，"自"的意思变为"自己"。"自"下面加上了（畀），念作 bi，指"鼻子"。

The original form of this character was 自, which has the shape of a nose. Pronounced as zi, it was later extended to mean "self". When 畀 (pronounced as bi) is placed below 自, it is pronounced as bi, meaning the nose. 畀 means to give. In breathing, one has to inhale and exhale, which is a form of give-and-take.

【部首】 Radical　　鼻(nose)

【同部首字】 Characters under the radical

鼾 （snore）

【词语】 Words and phrases

鼻窦	bídòu	paranasal sinus
鼻孔	bíkǒng	nostril
鼻腔	bíqiāng	nasal cavity
鼻塞	bísāi	have a stuffy nose
鼻祖	bízǔ	the earliest ancestor; originator (of a tradition, school of thought, etc.)
鼻烟壶	bíyānhú	snuff bottle

鼻渊　　　　　bíyuān　　　　nasosinusitis

鼻青脸肿
　　bí qīng liǎn zhǒng
　　　　a bloody nose and a swollen face
电光鼻镜
　　diàn guāng bí jìng
　　　　nasoscope
鹰钩鼻子
　　yīng gōu bí zi
　　　　aquiline nose; Roman nose

【例句】 Example
　　不要只顾鼻子底下的小事。
　　　　bú yào zhǐ gù bí zǐ dǐ xià de xiǎo shì
　　　　　Don't get bogged down in trivial matters.

biǎo

(surface; outside)

一　二　丰　圭　ヨ　表　表　表

"表"（）是由毛（屮）和衣（凸）组成的会意字。上面是毛发或毛皮大衣，而下面是"衣服"。古时人们爱穿用动物皮毛制成的毛衣，通常有毛的一边都会造在衣服的外面。

An ideogram composed of 衣 (clothes) and 毛 (hair). Written as"" in Little Zhuan, the upper part represents hair or fur and the lower part, clothes. The ancients used to wear animal fur to protect themselves against the cold. When they did so, the hairy side was always put on the outside. However, unless one is told, one can hardly discern the 毛 "" part of this character.

【部首】 Radical　　衣(clothes)(衤)

【同部首字】 Characters under the radical
袋(bag)，裁(judge)，装(clothes)

【词语】 Words and phrases

表白	biǎobái	vindicate
表层	biǎocéng	surface layer
表达	biǎodá	express; convey
表决	biǎojué	decide by vote
表露	biǎolù	show; reveal
表面	biǎomiàn	surface; outside appearance

| 表情 | biǎoqíng | expression |
| 表态 | biǎotài | make known one's position, declare where one stands |

表白诚意

    biǎo bái chéng yì

        assert one's sincerity

表里不一

    biǎo lǐ bù yī

        think in one way and behave in another

表面现象

    biǎo miàn xiàn xiàng

        superficial phenomenon

表明立场

    biǎo míng lì chǎng

        make known one's position

表现手法

    biǎo xiàn shǒu fǎ

        technique of expression

表意文字

    biǎo yì wén zì

        ideograph

【例句】Example

    我激动的心情难以用语言来表达。

        wǒ jī dòng de xīn qíng nán yǐ yòng yǔ yán lái biǎo dá

           Words can hardly express my excitement.

căi

(to pick)

这是一个会意字。在金文中，"采"（）由"手"（ᴧ）字和"木"（木）字组成，意思是"从树上采摘果实或树叶"。

An ideogram. In metal language "", it comprised of the hand "ᴧ" and tree "木" characters. By association, it indicates picking fruits or leaves on the tree.

【部首】 Radical   ᴧ (claw)

【同部首字】 Characters under the radical
　　觅 （look for），受 （accept）

【词语】 Words and phrases

采伐	căifá	fell; cut
采访	căifăng	interview
采购	căigòu	make purchases for an organization or enterprise
采集	căijí	gather; collect
采矿	căikuàng	mining
采用	căiyòng	adopt; use; employ
采择	căizé	select and adopt
采摘	căizhāi	pick

采录民歌

    cǎi lù mín gē

        collect and record folk songs

采取攻势

    cǎi qǔ gōng shì

        take the offensive

地下采矿

    dì xià cǎi kuàng

        underground mining

蒸汽采暖

    zhēng qì cǎi nuǎn

        steam heating

【例句】Example

    我们今天早晨去采集昆虫标本好吗?

        wǒ mén jīn tiān zǎo chén qù cǎi jí kūn chóng biāo běn hǎo ma

            Shall we go collecting insect specimen this morning?

册

cè

(volume; book)

丿 刀 刀 刑 册

你们知道在纸张还未发明前，中国人是用什么来写字的？答案是木片或竹片，为了方便收藏，它们的形状大小都是统一的。当木片、竹片排列在一起，中间用绳子连贯起来，就成了一本书（册）。

Pictogram. We know that before the invention of paper-making, ancient Chinese used to write on wooden or bamboo strips. The length and width of these strips, were standardised so that they could be tied together by a piece of string or ox-hide band. When this was done, a volume "册" was ready for use.

【部首】 Radical   一(horizontal line)

【同部首字】 Characters under the radical
丁(a surname), 干(do), 上(above)

【词语】 Words and phrases

册页	cèyè	an album of paintings or calligraphy
册子	cèzi	book; volume
画册	huàcè	picture album
纪念册	jìniàncè	album
名册	míngcè	namelist

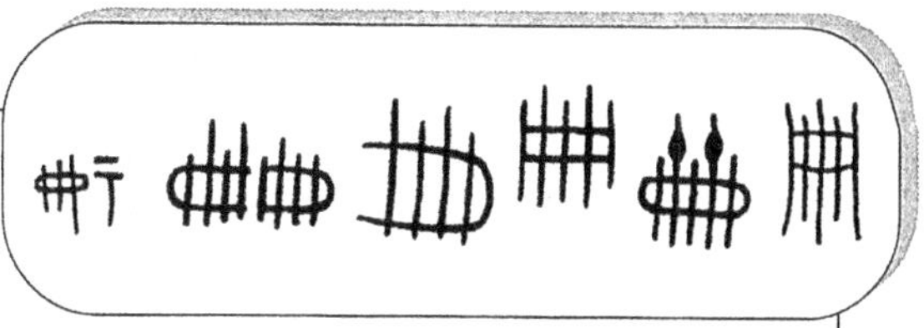

装订成册

　　zhuāng dīng chéng cè

　　　　bind into book form

载入史册

　　zǎi rù shǐ cè

　　　　go down in history

【例句】Example

　　这本书已销售十万册。

　　　　zhè běn shū yǐ xiāo shòu shí wàn cè

　　　　　　100,000 copies of the book have been sold.

cháo

(nest)

⸝	⸜⸜	⸝⸝⸝	⸜⸜⸜	凶	凷	凸	単	単	巣	巢

　　"巢"（）可分成三部分：上面是三只小鸟伸出头来（巛），中间是一个雀巢（臼），下面是一棵树（木）。所以"巢"就是指建在树上的鸟窝。

Pictogram. In Little Zhuan, the character was written as "巢", the top part "巛" representing three birds, the middle part "臼" a nest, and the lower part "木" a tree. As you might have guessed, the character means a bird nest on a tree.

【部首】 Radical　　巛 (river)

【词语】 Words and phrases

巢菜	cháocài	common vetch
巢蛾	cháo'é	ermine moth
巢鼠	cháoshǔ	harvest mouse
巢穴	cháoxuè	lair; den; nest; hideout
匪巢	fěicháo	nest (or den) of robbers; bandits lair
鸟巢	niǎocháo	bird's nest

雀巢咖啡
　　què cháo kā fēi
　　　　Nescafe

直捣巢穴

zhí dǎo cháo xuè

attack the enemy's lair; destroy the bandits' den

蜜蜂蜂巢

mì fēng fēng cháo

honeycomb

共筑爱巢

gòng zhù ài cháo

set up their own love nest

【例句】Example

再坏的鸟也不会弄脏自己的窝巢。

zài huài de niǎo yě bú huì nòng zāng zì jǐ de wō cháo

It is an ill bird that fouls his own nest.

车

chē

(chariot; car; vehicle)

一	生	车	车

以前的"车"（），下面的横线（）是车轴，（）是车架，左右两边（）是车轮，（）是马杆，组合成一辆马车，便是人们主要的交通工具。古时的马车多为两轮马车。

Pictogram. In metal language, it looked like a bird's-eye view of a vehicle "". The horizontal line "" at the bottom represents the axle, "" the carriage, the two vertical lines "" on its left and right the two wheels, and "" in front, shafts for the two horses or oxen. In ancient times, 车 generally meant two-wheeled chariots.

【部首】Radical   车(cart)

【同部首字】Characters under the radical
    较(compare)，轻(light)，输(lose)

【词语】Words and phrases

车道	chēdào	(traffic) lane
车队	chēduì	motorcade
车祸	chēhuò	traffic (or road) accident
车轮	chēlún	wheel (of a vehicle)
车票	chēpiào	train or bus ticket; ticket
车站	chēzhàn	station; depot; stop

车水马龙

　　chē shuǐ mǎ lóng

　　　　heavy traffic

车载斗量

　　chē zǎi dǒu liáng

　　　　enough to fill carts and be measured by the dou

　　　　　　i.e., common and numerous

来往车辆

　　lái wǎng chē liàng

　　　　traffic

装配车间

　　zhuāng pèi chē jiān

　　　　assembly shop

车到山前必有路

　　chē dào shān qián bì yǒu lù

　　　　The cart will find its way round the hill when it gets there.

　　　　　　i.e., Things will eventually sort themselves out.

【例句】Example

　　在我们这里像我这样的人车载斗量，不可胜数。

　　　　zài wǒ mén zhè lǐ xiàng wǒ zhè yàng de rén chē zǎi dǒu liáng, bù kě shèng shǔ

　　　　　Where I come from, people like me come by the bushel.

川

chuān

(river; waterway)

丿	川	川

你看甲骨文的"川"（ ），是不是很像一条河流呢？后来"川"字慢慢简化成三条弯曲的线（ ），使人一看便能联想到流水。

Pictogram. On oracle bones, it was " ", which indicates water flowing between river banks. In metal language, it evolved to three curved lines " ", giving a better presentation to the way water flows in a river.

【部首】 Radical　　丿 (left falling)

【同部首字】 Characters under the radical
久(long)，反(oppose)，九(nine)

【词语】 Words and phrases

川贝	chuānbèi	tendril-leaved fritillary bulb
川剧	chuānjù	Sichuan opera
川芎	chuānxiōng	the rhizome of Chuanxiong (Ligusticum wallichi)
川资	chuānzī	travelling expenses

高山大川
gāo shān dà chuān
　　high mountains and big rivers

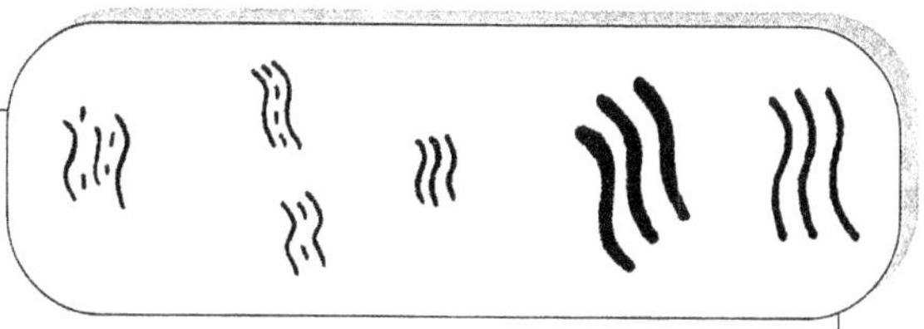

一马平川

　　yì mǎ píng chuān

　　　　a vast expanse of flat land; a great stretch of land

川流不息

　　chuān liú bù xī

　　　　flowing past in an endless stream

【例句】Example

　　在大川大海中锻炼自己。

　　　　zài dà chuān dà hǎi zhōng duàn liàn zì jǐ

　　　　　　Temper oneself in big rivers and seas.

大

dà

(big; great)

一 ナ 大

古时候，大字像手脚尽量伸开的人（），那是宽大和巨大的意思，一看它的象形图你就可感受到！

Pictogram. From oracle bones, we can see that "大" looked like the frontal view of a man who is stretching his arms and legs to the limit in order to demonstrate his breadth. The character therefore means "great and broad".

【部首】 Radical 　　　大(big)

【同部首字】 Characters under the radical
　　　奇(strange)，夹(clip)，夫(husband)

【词语】 Words and phrases

大败	dàbài	defeat utterly; put to rout
大肠	dàcháng	large intestine
大潮	dàcháo	spring tide
大胆	dàdǎn	bold; daring
大刀	dàdāo	broadsword
大方	dàfang	generous; liberal; easy
大楼	dàlóu	multi-storied building

大笔一挥

dà bǐ yì huī

 with one stroke of the pen

大慈大悲

dà cí dà bēi

 infinitely merciful

大发雷霆

dà fā léi tíng

 be furious; fly into a rage; bawl at sb. angrily

大功告成

dà gōng gào chéng

 (of a project, work, etc.) be accomplished; be crowned with success

大惑不解

dà huò bù jiě

 be extremely puzzled; be unable to make head or tail of sth.

大千世界

dà qiān shì jiè

 the boundless universe

大失所望

dà shī suǒ wàng

 greatly disappointed; to one's great disappointment

大义灭亲

dà yì miè qīn

 place righteousness above family loyalty

大事化小，小事化了

dà shì huà xiǎo, xiǎo shì huà liǎo

 down play a problem or ignore it altogether

【例句】 Example

这种料子的颜色和花样很大方。

 zhè zhǒng liào zǐ de yán sè hé huā yàng hěn dà fāng

  The pattern and colour of this fabric are in good taste.

旦

dàn

(sunrise)

"旦"（♀）的结构很简单，只有两部分：太阳（☉）和地平线（◖），让人一看便猜出是太阳从地面升起的样子。

Ideogram. It was written like this "♀" on oracle bones. The top part "☉" represents the sun, and the symbol below "◖" the earth. When the sun emerges from the earth, it is of course sunrise.

【部首】Radical   日(sun)

【同部首字】Characters under the radical
　　旱(draught)，智(wise)，暖(warm)

【词语】Words and phrases

一旦	yídàn	in a single day; once; in case
元旦	Yuándàn	New Year's Day
旦角	dànjué	female role in Peking Opera
旦暮	dànmù	day and night; in a short period of time
旦夕	dànxī	morning and evening; in a short while

旦夕之间

    dàn xī zhī jiān

        in a day's time; overnight

危在旦夕

    wēi zài dàn xī

        in imminent danger

旦不保夕

    dàn bù bǎo xī

        face instant danger; in a precarious situation

旦暮入地

    dàn mù rù dì

        with one leg in the grave

通宵达旦

    tōng xiāo dá dàn

        all night long; all through the night

【例句】Example

    他们相处多年，一旦分别，不免依依不舍。

        tā mén xiāng chǔ duō nián, yí dàn fēn bié, bù miǎn yī yī bù shě

            After being together for years, they can't bear to part from each other.

岛

dǎo

(island)

′	㇆	勹	鸟	鸟	岛	岛

形声字。由（🐦）和（⼭）两个字组合而成。古人认为，从海上突出来的陆地就是山。把小鸟的喳喳声和海浪声加进去就形成了"岛"字。

Pictophonetic character. Formed by combining the characters bird "🐦" and mountain "⼭". The ancients considered that which emerged from the surface of the sea a mountain. By merging the chirping of the birds with the sound of splashing waves, the character 岛 is created.

【部首】 Radical   ⼭(mountain)

【同部首字】 Characters under the radical
　　岁（age）, 岭（mountain range）, 岳（high mountain）

【词语】 Words and phrases

安全岛	ānquándǎo	safety island; pedestrian island
岛国	dǎoguó	country consisting of one or more islands; island country
岛屿	dǎoyǔ	islands and islets; islands
孤岛	gūdǎo	desert island
小岛	xiǎodǎo	small island

岛上居民

dǎo shàng jū mín

islander

越岛作战

yuè dǎo zuò zhàn

island hopping

【例句】 Example

他受困于荒岛之上。

tā shòu kùn yú huāng dǎo zhī shàng

He was marooned on a deserted island.

dé

(virtue)

丿 ㇇ 彳 彳 彳 彳 彳 彳 彳 德 德 德 德 德 德

德这个字右边中间的部分，不是"四"字，而是一个横放了的"目"字。所以是"十目一"组成的"直"字，"直"字再加上"心"，便是正直的心。而"德行"就是叫我们不要做坏事，只做好事和善事，成为一个品德高尚的人。"做"是要"行动"的，所以用了"彳"来做部首。你平时注重自己的品德吗？

An ideogram. That which is straight-forward and comes from the heart is virtuous 德, i.e., say what you feel and do what you think is right. In this character, the 直 (meaning straight) component is turned sideways "罒" while retaining the horizontal line below, which makes it look like this "罒". So from now on, please don't forget the horizontal line when you write the character 德.

【部首】Radical　　　彳 (step)

【同部首字】Characters under the radical
往(go)，彷(mooch)，很(very)

【词语】Words and phrases

德国	Déguó	Germany
德行	déxíng	moral conduct
德语	Déyǔ	German (language)
德育	déyù	moral education

| 德政 | dézhèng | benevolent rule |
| 德治 | dézhì | rule of virtue |

同心同德

    tóng xīn tóng dé

        be of one heart and one mind

德才兼备

    dé cái jiān bèi

        have both ability and political integrity

德高望重

    dé gāo wàng zhòng

        be of noble character and hight prestige; enjoy high prestige and command universal respect

以怨报德

    yǐ yuàn bào dé

        return evil for good; repay kindness with ingratitude; bite the hand that feeds you

【例句】Example

    那个家伙真德行。

    nà gè jiā huǒ zhēn dé xíng

        That fellow is really disgusting.

的

dì

(bull's-eye)

′	亻	白	白	白	白	的	的

这是一个象形字，由"白"和"勺"组成。靶子中央的白点就是靶心，"勺"代表它周围的圆环。射手射中靶心叫作"中的"。射箭时眼睛要盯住靶心，所以产生了"目的"这个词。

Pictogram, composed of 白 (white) and 勺(spoon). In archery, the white spot in the centre of the target is the bull's-eye and 勺 indicates the circle around it. Notice it has a dot in the centre. When the archer's arrow hits the bull's-eye, he is said to have 中的. Usually, in an archery context, you have your eye 目 fixed on the bull's-eye, that is how the expression 目的 (purpose) came into use.

【部首】 Radical   白(white)

【同部首字】 Characters under the radical
泉(spring)，皆(all)，皎(clear and bright)

【词语】 Words and phrases

的确	díquè	indeed; really
目的	mùdì	purpose; aim; goal; objective
目的地	mùdìdì	destination

目的明确

　　mù dì míng què

　　　have a definite purpose

无的放矢

　　wú dì fàng shǐ

　　　shoot an arrow without a target; shoot at random

众矢之的

　　zhòng shǐ zhī dì

　　　target of public criticism (or censure)

【例句】Example

　　他们安全抵达了目的地。

　　　tā mén ān quán dǐ dá le mù dì dì

　　　　They arrived at the destination safely.

斗

dǒu

(a vessel with a handle; a weight unit)

、	ニ	三	斗

斗（𣂏）就是古代的器皿，它的上面是容器或器皿（つ），下面是容器的手柄（𠂉）。它后来发展成中国特有的一种量器以及容量单位。你听过"不为五斗米而折腰"这句话吗？

Pictogram. In metal language, it was written as "𣂏", the top part "つ" showing a vessel and the lower part "𠂉" its handle. That is exactly what it means. By implication, it becomes a weight unit.

【部首】Radical   斗(a vessel)

【同部首字】Characters under the radical
　　料(material)，斜(oblique)，斟(pour)

【词语】Words and phrases

斗胆	dǒudǎn	make bold
斗拱	dǒugǒng	dougong, a system of brackets inserted between the top of column and a crossbeam (each bracket being formed of a double bow-shaped arm, called gong, which supports a block of wood, called dou, in each side)
斗笠	dǒulì	bamboo hat
斗篷	dǒupeng	cape; cloak
斗渠	dǒuqú	lateral canal

斗室	dǒushì	a samll room
漏斗	lòudǒu	funnel
烟斗	yāndǒu	(tobacco) pipe

斗米尺布

    dǒu mǐ chǐ bù

        little food and cloth

斗转星移

    dǒu zhuǎn xīng yí

        the day dawns

斗酒只鸡

    dǒu jiǔ zhī jī

        simple meal; to commemorate the death of a dear one with wine and chicken

车载斗量

    chē zǎi dǒu liáng

        enough to fill carts and be measured by the dou

            i,e., common and numerous

【例句】 Example

    我斗胆说一句，这件事您做错了。

        wǒ dǒu dǎn shuō yí jù, zhè jiàn shì nín zuò cuò le

        May I make bold to suggest that you were wrong to do so?

斗

dòu

(tussle; fight)

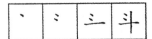

从这个象形字的甲骨文中我们可以看出两个正在打斗的人（㺵），胳膊交叉（ㄨ），这也正是这个字的本义。后来又引申出"竞赛"、"竞争"的意思。

Pictogram. From the symbol "㺵" on oracle bones, we can distinguish two men engaged in a fight, their arms "ㄨ" locked in a tussle. Hence fighting against each other. By extension, it also means a contest.

【部首】 Radical　　斗(fight)

【同部首字】 Characters under the radical
　　料(material)，斜(oblique)，斟(pour)

【词语】 Words and phrases

斗鸡	dòujī	gamecock; cockfighting
斗气	dòuqì	quarrel or contend with sb. on account or a personal grudge
斗眼	dòuyǎn	cross-eye
斗争	dòuzhēng	struggle; fight; combat
斗志	dòuzhì	will to fight
斗智	dòuzhì	battle of wits

斗智昂扬

    dòu zhì áng yáng

        have high morale

鼓舞斗志

    gǔ wǔ dòu zhì

        arouse the fighting will

斗鸡走狗

    dòu jī zǒu gǒu

        cock fight and dog race, an ancient form of Chinese gambling somewhat like horse-racing

【例句】Example

虽然屡遭败绩，他们仍甚有斗志。

    suī rán lǚ zāo bài jì, tā mén réng shèn yǒu dòu zhì

        In spite of numerous defeats, they still had plenty of fight left in them.

儿

ér

(child; son)

丿 | 儿

看看甲骨文的"儿"字（），像不像一个小孩子？上半部分是一个小孩子的脑袋（ᴗ），下半部分是一个人（⺅），所以这个字的模样就告诉我们："儿"是"一个小孩"。

Pictograph. In oracle bones "", the lower part is a person "⺅" and the upper part a human head "ᴗ", with the fontanel not yet fully developed. This indicates he is still a child.

【部首】Radical   儿(son)

【同部首字】Characters under the radical
元(initial)，光(light)，先(first)

【词语】Words and phrases

儿歌	érgē	children's song; nursery rhymes
儿科	érkē	(department of) paediatrics
儿女	érnǚ	sons and daughters
儿孙	érsūn	children and grandchildren; descendants; posterity
儿童	értóng	children
儿媳	érxí	daughter-in-law
儿戏	érxì	trifling matter
儿子	érzi	son

儿科医生

    ér kē yī shēng

        paediatrician

儿女情长

    ér nǚ qíng cháng

        be immersed in love

儿童读物

    ér tóng dú wù

        children's books

儿童医院

    ér tóng yī yuàn

        children's hospital

英雄儿女

    yīng xióng ér nǚ

        young heroes and heroines

【例句】Example

    他有一儿一女。

        tā yǒu yì ér yì nǚ

        He has a son and a daughter.

犯

fàn

(criminal)

ノ	犭	犭	犯	犯

　　这个字的左边有一只"狗"（犭），右边有一个坐着的人（卩）。古时，狗的职责就是要看守着犯人，不让他趁机逃走。相信只有囚犯才会被狗监视着！

　　"犬"（犭）on the left is the symbol for a dog; "卩" on the right originally looked like "卩", which represents a person seated. The meaning of this character is derived from the situation when a criminal is tired from standing a long time, he is allowed to sit down, but a dog is called in to keep watch on him.

【部首】 Radical　　犭 (dog)

【同部首字】 Characters under the radical
　　狗(dog)，狂(crazy)，狠(ruthless)

【词语】 Words and phrases

犯案	fàn'àn	be found out and brought to justice
犯病	fànbìng	have an attack of one's old illness
犯不着	fànbuzháo	not worthwhile
犯愁	fànchóu	worry; be anxious
犯法	fànfǎ	violate (or break) the law
犯规	fànguī	break the rules
犯忌	fànjì	violate a taboo

犯人	fànrén	prisoner
犯罪	fànzuì	commit a crime (or an offence)

犯法行为

    fàn fǎ xíng wéi

        offence against the law

犯罪分子

    fàn zuì fèn zǐ

        offender; criminal

犯罪行为

    fàn zuì xíng wéi

        criminal offence

侵人犯规

    qīn rén fàn guī

        personal foul

【例句】 Example

    他的气喘病又犯了。

        tā de qì chuǎn bìng yòu fàn le

            He's got another attack of asthma.

fēi

(imperial concubine; princess)

由 "女" 和 "己" 组成的 "妃"，原本指男人的妻子，他们会很自豪地说："这是我的妻子！" 后来，人们才把在皇宫里与皇帝有关系的女人叫作 "妃子"，当然，这不包括皇后。

This ideogram has two parts. The left being a woman 女 and the right self 己. Originally, 妃 meant a man's wife, implying that "the woman is mine." Later it became a special term for the emperor's concubines who ranked next to the queen.

【部首】Radical 　　女(female)

【同部首字】Characters under the radical
　　娘(mother)，姻(marriage)，好(good)

【词语】Words and phrases

妃嫔	fēipín	imperial concubines of all ranks
妃子	fēizi	imperial concubine
贵妃	guìfēi	imperial concubine of the highest rank
王妃	wángfēi	princess

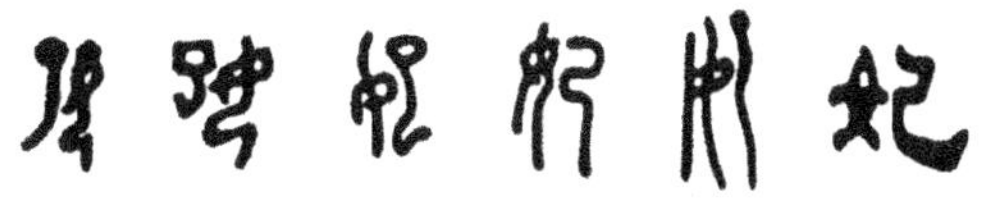

贵妃醉酒

guì fēi zuì jiǔ

The Drunken Beauty, a Peking Opera about an emperor and his favourite concubine

【例句】Example

在古代，中国皇帝有三宫六院七十二妃。

zài gǔ dài, zhōng guó huáng dì yǒu sān gōng liù yuàn qī shí èr fēi

In ancient times, Chinese emperors had three empresses, six high-ranking imperial concubines and seventy-two ordinary concubines.

fēi

(wrong; no)

丿	刁	刂	刂	刲	非	非	非

　　以前跟"飞"字是同一来源的，看上去就像雀鸟展翅飞翔的样子（非）。随着时代转变，它竟变成了"是非"的"非"，有"相反"和"违背"的意思，还有"异常"的意思。

Pictogram. This character was originally a homophone and synonym of the character 飞. From metal language "非", we can detect a bird flapping its wings. However, as the Chinese language developed, this character lost its original meaning and came to mean "wrong" in the expression 是非 (right and wrong), and "unusually" or "abnormal" in the expression 非常.

【部首】 Radical　　　| (vertical line)

【同部首字】 Characters under the radical
　　师(teacher)，旧(old)，出(out)

【词语】 Words and phrases

非常	fēicháng	extraordinary; unusual; special
非但	fēidàn	not only
非法	fēifǎ	illegal; unlawful; illicit
非凡	fēifán	outstanding; extraordinary; uncommon
非分	fēifèn	overstepping one's bounds; assuming
非命	fēimìng	die a violent death

| 非难 | fēinàn | blame; censure, reproach |
| 非议 | fēiyì | reproach; censure |

非比寻常
> fēi bǐ xún cháng
>> unusual

非亲非故
> fēi qīn fēi gù
>> neither relative nor friend; neither kith nor kin

非此即彼
> fēi cǐ jí bǐ
>> either this or that; one or the other

非公莫入
> fēi gōng mò rù
>> no admittance except on business

非同小可
> fēi tóng xiǎo kě
>> no small (or trivial) matter

分清是非
> fēn qīng shì fēi
>> distinguish between right and wrong

为非作歹
> wéi fēi zuò dǎi
>> do evil

【例句】Example

他非但自己干得好，还肯帮助别人。
> tā fēi dàn zì jǐ gàn de hǎo, hái kěn bāng zhù bié rén
>> He not only does his own work well, but is also ready to help others.

fèn

(lift oneself; exert oneself)

一 ナ 大 大 夲 夯 奋 奋

这个字最初写作（𡙟）。下半部的（⊕）代表土地。上半部（𨾫）是一只挥动翅膀的鸟。一只鸟要想高飞需要奋力，因此这个字的本义是"提升自己"，引申为"振作"。

Pictogram. In its original form, this character was written as "𡙟". The lower part "⊕" represents the land, or the ground. The upper part "𨾫" is a bird with its wings flapping. A bird in rapid ascent needs to make an effort, therefore this character means "to lift oneself" and by extension, "act vigorously".

【部首】Radical 　　大(big)

【同部首字】Characters under the radical
奔(run)，夸(praise)，牵(lead)

【词语】Words and phrases

奋斗	fèndòu	struggle; fight; strive
奋发	fènfā	rouse oneself; exert oneself
奋力	fènlì	do all one can
奋勉	fènmiǎn	make a determined effort
奋起	fènqǐ	rise with force and spirit
奋勇	fènyǒng	summon up all one's courage and energy
奋战	fènzhàn	fight bravely

奋起直追

　　fèn qǐ zhí zhuī

　　　do all one can to catch up

奋斗到底

　　fèn dòu dào dǐ

　　　fight to the bitter end

奋不顾身

　　fèn bú gù shēn

　　　dash ahead regardless of one's safety

奋发图强

　　fèn fā tú qiáng

　　　go all out to make the country strong; work hard for the prosperity of
　　　the country

【例句】 Example

　　骑兵战士冲入敌群，奋力砍杀。

　　　qí bīng zhàn shì chōng rù dí qún, fèn lì kǎn shā

　　　　The cavalrymen charged into the enemy ranks, slashing furiously.

福

fú

(good fortune; happiness; blessing)

| ` | 丿 | 礻 | 礻 | 礻 | 礻 | 衤 | 衤 | 衤 | 禑 | 褔 | 褔 | 福 |

形声字。古时候这个字写作（禑）。左边的（🍶）是一个酒坛，右边的（示）代表祭祖或祭天用的祭品。古代人上供时要把酒洒在地上，他们相信这样会带来好运。

Pictophonetic character. In ancient times, the character was written as "禑". The "🍶"on the right depicts a wine flask while "示" on the left represents offering to the ancestors or heaven. When the ancients made offerings, they sprinkled wine on the ground, believing this would bring good luck to themselves.

【部首】 Radical　　礻(indicate)

【同部首字】 Characters under the radical
礼(rite)，祖(ancestor)，神(god)

【词语】 Words and phrases

福分	fúfen	good fortune
福利	fúlì	material benefits; well-being; welfare
福气	fúqi	happy lot; good fortune
福星	fúxīng	lucky star; mascot
福音	fúyīn	Gospel; glad tidings

福利设施

　　fú lì shè shī

　　　　welfare facilities

福利事业

　　fú lì shì yè

　　　　welfare projects (or services)

造福人类

　　zào fú rén lèi

　　　　promote the well-being of mankind

【例句】Example

　　你可不能身在福中不知福啊!

　　　　nǐ kě bù néng shēn zài fú zhōng bù zhī fú a

　　　　　　Don't take your good fortune for granted.

gāo

(lamb; kid)

丶	⼶	⼷	⼸	⽺	羊	羊	羔	羔	羔

　　从羔（羔）的字形，你能猜到其中意思吗？上面是一只羊（羊），下面是火（火），合起来就是指"烤羊肉"，后来解作小羊。古时的人还真聪明，早已知道烤羊肉是很有特色的美食了。

　　An ideogram. We can almost guess what it means just by looking at its original form "羔". The upper part "羊" symboliscs a sheep and the lower part "火" a fire, indicating the roasting of mutton. The ancient Chinese already knew that barbecued mutton was especially delicious. Later on , 羔 came to mean simply lamb.

【部首】Radical　　　羊 (sheep)

【同部首字】Characters under the radical
　　羡 (envy)，羞 (shy)，羚 (antelope)

【词语】Words and phrases

羔皮	gāopí	lambskin; kidskin; kid
羔羊	gāoyáng	lamb; kid
羔子	gāozi	lamb; kid; fawn

羊羔皮革

     yáng gāo pí gé

       leather made from a lambskin

【例句】Example

    房屋后有一些羊羔。

      fáng wū hòu yǒu yì xiē yáng gāo

        There are some lambs behind the house.

公

gōng

(fair; just)

丿 | 八 | 公 | 公

在一只开口的瓶子（ㄷ）上方平均地摆放着一些东西（）（），就是指"公"（㞷）。它有着"平均"、"公正"、"公平分配"的意思。如果人人都奉公守法，我们便会拥有一个公平、公正的社会。

Pictogram. In metal language, it was written as "㞷". The lower part "ㄷ" represents an open jar while "）（" on the top represents even distribution of the stuff inside. Hence the meaning "fair" or "just".

【部首】 Radical　　　八(eight)

【同部首字】 Characters under the radical
　　其(that)，兵(soldier)

【词语】 Words and phrases

公案	gōng'àn	a legal case
公布	gōngbù	promulgate; announce; publish; make public
公道	gōngdao	fair; just; reasonable; impartial
公德	gōngdé	social morality; social ethics
公敌	gōngdí	public enemy
公开	gōngkāi	open, overt; public
公理	gōnglǐ	generally acknowledged truth; self-evident truth

公众　　　　　gōngzhòng　　　the public

私设公堂

　　sī shè gōng táng

　　　　set up an illegal court

公共设施

　　gōng gòng shè shī

　　　　public utilities

公诸同好

　　gōng zhū tóng hào

　　　　share enjoyment with those of the same taste

公之于世

　　gōng zhī yú shì

　　　　make known to the world; reveal to the public

买卖公平

　　mǎi mài gōng píng

　　　　be fair in buying and selling; buy and sell at reasonable prices

公报私仇

　　gōng bào sī chóu

　　　　avenge a personal wrong in the name of public interest; abuse public
　　　　power to retaliate on personal enemy

【例句】Example

　我还有很多公事要办。

　　wǒ hái yǒu hěn duō gōng shì yào bàn

　　　　I still have a lot of official duties to attend to.

寡

guǎ

(alone; few)

丶 宀 宀 宀 宀 宀 宂 宆 宆 宣 宣 寡 寡 寡

　　这个会意字包括两部分，上半部的（宀）表示房屋，下面是被拆分成上下两部分的"颁"字，表示"分离"。如果一个人和同伴分开，独自呆在屋子里，他一定很孤独。

Ideogram consisting of two parts. The top "宀" represents a house or a room, underneath it is 颁 split into two parts, one placed on top of the other to form "寡". The accent here is separation. Just as the two parts are separated, when a person is separated from his peers and kept in a house all by himself, he is alone.

【部首】 Radical　　　宀(roof)

【同部首字】 Characters under the radical
　　宾(guest)，完(finish)

【词语】 Words and phrases

寡妇	guǎfù	widow
寡人	guǎrén	I, the sovereign; we
寡头	guǎtóu	oligarch
鳏寡	guānguǎ	widowers and widows
守寡	shǒuguǎ	live in widowhood

寡不敌众

　　guǎ bù dí zhòng

　　　　be hopelessly outnumbered

寡廉鲜耻

　　guǎ lián xiǎn chǐ

　　　　shameless

沉默寡言

　　chén mò guǎ yán

　　　　uncommunicative; taciturn

失道寡助

　　shī dào guǎ zhù

　　　　An unjust cause finds scant support.

以寡敌众

　　yǐ guǎ dí zhòng

　　　　pit the few against the many; fight against heavy odds

【例句】Example

　　她是一位孤寡老人。

　　　　tā shì yí wèi gū guǎ lǎo rén

　　　　　　She is a lonely old lady.

guān

(close; shut)

丶	丷	丷	兰	关	关

这个形声字的外面是门，里面是（丱）。古时门是用两块木板做成的，把两块木板立在一起，用绳子拴住，门就关好了。后来这个字简化成我们现在写的样子。

Pictophonetic character, it is composed of 门, the symbol for door, on the outside and "丱", symbolising pieces of string, within. In ancient times, the door was made up of two wooden planks. After they were put together and tied with pieces of string, the door was securely shut.

【部首】 Radical   丷 (eight)

【同部首字】 Characters under the radical
并 (combine)， 半 (half)

【词语】 Words and phrases

关闭	guānbì	close; shut
关怀	guānhuái	show loving care for; show solicitude for
关键	guānjiàn	hinge; key; crux
关门	guānmén	close
关切	guānqiè	be deeply concerned; show one's concern over
关税	guānshuì	customs duty; tariff
关系	guānxi	relation; relationship

关照　　　　　　guānzhào　　　look after;
　　　　　　　　　　　　　　　　keep an eye on

关怀备至
　　guān huái bèi zhì
　　　　show the utmost solicitude
关键时刻
　　guān jiàn shí kè
　　　　a critical (or crucial) moment
关门打狗
　　guān mén dǎ gǒu
　　　　bolt the door and beat the dog
　　　　　　i.e., block the enemy's retreat and then destroy him
紧要关头
　　jǐn yào guān tóu
　　　　a critical moment
外交关系
　　wài jiāo guān xì
　　　　diplomatic relations

【例句】 Example
　　别把孩子整天关在家里。
　　　　bié bǎ hái zǐ zhěng tiān guān zài jiā lǐ
　　　　　　Don't keep the children inside all day.

guān

(officials)

丶	丷	宀	宁	宁	宁	官	官

　　从官（官）字的结构来看，（宀）是一间房屋，（𠂤）是民众，合起来就有了"政府机构"或"办公室"的意义，后来又多了"官员"、"官吏"的含义。

In metal language, "官" is composed of "宀" and "𠂤". The latter represents the masses while the former a house. Put together, they depict a house which is used for administering the people, i.e., an administration office or government building. By extension, this character has come to mean government officials.

【部首】 Radical　　宀(roof)

【同部首字】 Characters under the radical
　　宇(house)，守(guard)，宿(stay overnight)

【词语】 Words and phrases

官邸	guāndǐ	official residence; official mansion
官价	guānjià	official price (or rate)
官吏	guānlì	government officials
官僚	guānliáo	bureaucrat
官腔	guānqiāng	bureaucratic tone
官司	guānsi	lawsuit
官职	guānzhí	government post; official position

官官相护

    guān guān xiāng hù

        Bureaucrats shield one another.

官僚主义

    guān liáo zhǔ yì

        bureaucracy

官样文章

    guān yàng wén zhāng

        mere formalities; officialese

官复原职

    guān fù yuan zhí

        restore an official to his original post; be reinstated

【例句】 Example

    这人真官僚。

        zhè rén zhēn guān liáo

        What a bureaucrat that fellow is.

guó

(country; nation)

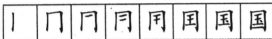

　　"国"字原本写作（或）（或），有三部分：（戈）是古代兵器；（ロ）是口，又指人民；（ノ）是土地，这三样都是组成国家的基本要素。从前，人们过着游牧的生活，没有划分特定的居住边界。经过战乱后，人们开始懂得为自己的土地筑起边界，于是在"或"加上"口"成为了"国"，也和"或"分开了用途。

　　Ideogram. We find in oracle bones the initial form of this character "或", "戈" represents a dagger-axe, an ancient weapon; " ロ " a mouth and by extension people and " ノ " land. These were the three essential factors for the formation of a country, underlining the importance of protecting with arms the land and people from outside invasion. People in primitive society were pastoral and therefore their tribal organisations had no fixed territory or boundary. After many armed clashes, they gradually learned to set up defences around what they considered their land. By then, this character changed to " 國 " and still later to 国. Notice here the boundary is fixed; instead of with one side open, it is now closed. That is how the character for country is written now.

【部首】 Radical　　□(enclosure)

【同部首字】 Characters under the radical
　　围(enclose)，团(group)，图(map)

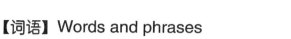

【词语】 Words and phrases

国宝	guóbǎo	national treasure
国宾	guóbīn	state guest
国耻	guóchǐ	national humiliation
国粹	guócuì	the quintessence of Chinese culture
国画	guóhuà	traditional Chinese painting
国籍	guójí	nationality

国际贸易

guó jì mào yì

international trade

国计民生

guó jì mín shēng

the national economy and the people's livelihood

国际收支

guó jì shōu zhī

balance of (international) payments

国家元首

guó jiā yuán shǒu

head of state

国际主义

guó jì zhǔ yì

internationalism

【例句】 Example

在中国，妇女和儿童受国家保护。

zài zhōng guó, fù nǚ hé ér tóng shòu guó jiā bǎo hù

In China, women and children are protected by the state.

果

guǒ

(fruit)

| 丶 | 冂 | 冂 | 日 | 旦 | 甲 | 畀 | 果 |

甲骨文的"果"是这样的（），可以看到树上有三个果实；而金文的"果"就是一个大大的果实（）。

A pictogram indicating fruits grown on a tree. On oracle bones, it was written as " ", which shows a tree with three fruits. In metal language, instead of three fruits " ", there is only one, but it is much bigger " ".

【部首】 Radical 木(tree)

【同部首字】 Characters under the radical
架(frame)，柳(willow)，枯(withered)

【词语】 Words and phrases

果断	guǒduàn	resolute; decisive
果脯	guǒfǔ	preserved fruit; candied fruit
果敢	guǒgǎn	courageous and resolute
果酱	guǒjiàng	jam
果木	guǒmù	fruit tree
果然	guǒrán	really; as expected; sure enough
果园	guǒyuán	orchard
果真	guǒzhēn	really

办事果断

    bàn shì guǒ duàn

        handle affairs in a decisive manner

果实累累

    guǒ shí lěi lěi

        fruit growing in close clusters; fruit hanging heavy on the trees

果树栽培

    guǒ shù zāi péi

        fruit growing; pomiculture

开花结果

    kāi huā jiē guǒ

        blossom and bear fruit

【例句】Example

    她果敢地跳入水中，救起溺水的孩子。

        tā guǒ gǎn de tiào rù shuǐ zhōng, jiù qǐ nì shuǐ de hái zǐ

            Without hesitation, she leapt into the water and saved the drowning child.

hán

(cold)

| 丶 | 宀 | 宀 | 宁 | 宁 | 宇 | 审 | 宯 | 寀 | 寅 | 寒 | 寒 |

"寒"（）的结构还真复杂呢！它被分成四个部分：屋（冂）、干草堆（艹）、男人（夲）、冰（仌），拼合起来就可看到一个男人睡在屋子里的干草堆上，草堆下全是冰，冷得让人发抖。

The way this character "☒" looked in Little Zhuan was rather complicated. However, one can still distinguish its four components. A room or hut "冂", a haystack "艹", a man "夲" and ice "仌". From this combination, we can conclude that a man is sleeping in a haystack in a room, but underneath the haystack is ice. It must be very cold indeed.

【部首】Radical 　　宀(roof)

【同部首字】Characters under the radical
　　密(secret)，寐(sleep)，寂(silent)

【词语】Words and phrases

寒潮	háncháo	cold current
寒碜	hánchen	ugly; unsightly
寒带	hándài	cold zone
寒流	hánliú	cold wave
寒气	hánqì	cold air; cold draught
寒酸	hánsuān	(of a poor scholar in the old days) miserable and shabby

寒心	hánxīn	be bitterly disappointed
寒衣	hányī	winter clothing
寒战	hánzhàn	shiver (with cold or fear)

寒冬腊月

   hán dōng là yuè

     severe winter; dead of winter

寒风刺骨

   hán fēng cì gǔ

     The cold wind chilled one to the bone.

寒来暑往

   hán lái shǔ wǎng

     as summer goes and winter comes; with the passage of time

寒气逼人

   hán qì bī rén

     There is a nip in the air.

天寒地冻

   tiān hán dì dòng

     The weather is cold and the ground is frozen.

【例句】Example

   初春季节仍有寒意。

     chū chūn jì jié réng yǒu hán yì

       It's spring but there's still a chill in the air.

hé

(fit; combine)

| 丿 | 人 | 亼 | 今 | 合 | 合 |

"合" 字（）的上面是一个镂盖（亼），下面是容器（廿）。把镂盖放在容器上面，就有了合口、结合的意思了。

In metal language, this ideogram looked like "合". The upper part is the lid of an urn or a pot "亼", and the lower part the container itself "廿". When the cover fits the pot, it means combine.

【部首】 Radical   口(mouth)

【同部首字】 Characters under the radical
    另(other)，唱(sing)，喝(drink)

【词语】 Words and phrases

合抱	hébào	(of a tree, etc.) so big that one can just get one's arms around
合并	hébìng	merge; amalgamate
合唱	héchàng	chorus
合成	héchéng	compose; compound
合法	héfǎ	legal; lawful; legitimate; rightful
合格	hégé	qualified; up to standard
合欢	héhuān	silk tree
合理	hélǐ	rational; reasonable; equitable

| 合同 | hétong | contract |
| 合意 | héyì | suit; be to one's liking (or taste) |

合情合理

hé qíng hé lǐ

fair and reasonable; fair and sensible

合影留念

hé yǐng liú niàn

have a group photo taken to mark the occasion

合作经济

hé zuò jīng jì

cooperative economy; cooperative sector of the economy

合二而一

hé èr ér yī

Two combine into one.

【例句】 Example

这幅画是他们合作的。

zhè fú huà shì tā mén hé zuò de

This painting is their joint work.

贺

hè

(festive; congratulate)

フ	カ	カ	加	加	加	贺	贺	贺

这个形声字由"加"和"贝"组成。"加"表示"增加","贝"是原始社会的货币。如果已经有了很多钱，亲戚朋友又来送礼，这当然是值得庆贺的事情。

Pictophonetic character composed of 加 and 贝. The top part means to increase, and the lower part is the symbol for shell, which was the currency used in primitive society. When one already has plenty of money, and one's friends and relatives come along with gifts, that increases his belongings, hence a festive or congratulatory occasion.

【部首】Radical　　贝(shell)

【同部首字】Characters under the radical
财(wealth)，贪(greedy)，购(purchase)

【词语】Words and phrases

贺词	hècí	speech (or message) of congratulation; congratulations; greetings
贺电	hèdiàn	message of congratulation; congratulatory telegram
贺礼	hèlǐ	gift (as a token of congratulation)
贺年	hènián	extend New Year greetings or pay a New Year call
贺喜	hèxǐ	congratulate sb. on a happy occasion (e.g. a wedding, the brith of a child, etc.)

贺信   hèxìn   letter of congratulation

恭贺新禧

gōng hè xīn xǐ

Happy New Year.

庆贺新年

qìng hè xīn nián

to greet or celebrate the New Year

【例句】 Example

我对你的成功致以最热烈的祝贺。

wǒ duì nǐ de chéng gōng zhì yǐ zuì rè liè de zhù hè

I send you my warmest congratulations on your success.

huī

(ash)

"灰"（）的字形很有趣，上面是一只手（），下面是火（火），就是说人们在火中取东西。被火烧伤是很痛的，所以人们会等火熄灭后才取东西，这时它已变成灰了。

In metal language, this ideogram was written as "灵". A hand "彐" on top and a fire "火" below, indicating the act of taking something out of the fire. When you pick something out from a fire, you don t want to burn yourself. You have to wait for the fire to die out. By that time all that is left are the ashes.

【部首】Radical　　火(fire)

【同部首字】Characters under the radical
　　炸(fry)，灯(lamp)，烘(bake)

【词语】Words and phrases

灰暗	huī'àn	murky grey; gloomy
灰白	huībái	greyish white; ashen;pale
灰溜溜	huīliūliū	gloomy; dejected; crestfallen
灰蒙蒙	huīméngméng	dusky; overcast
灰色	huīsè	grey; ashy; pessimistic; gloomy
灰心	huīxīn	lose heart; be discouraged

灰心丧气

    huī xīn sàng qì

      be utterly disheartened

化为灰烬

    huà wéi huī jìn

      be reduced to ashes

心灰意懒

    xīn huī yì lǎn

      fell disheartened

成功不骄傲，失败不灰心

    chéng gōng bù jiāo ào, shī bài bù huī xīn

      When you succeed don't get conceited; when you fail don't be dejected.

【例句】Example

    大风过后，桌子上落了一层灰。

      dà fēng guò hòu, zhuō zǐ shàng luò le yì céng huī

        After the wind, there was a layer of dust on the desk.

监

jiān

(scrutinise)

丶	刂	丬	丬	刂丶	刂丶	丬丶	丬丶	监	监

　　会意字。这个字在金文中写作（盥）。左上角的图形（ϵ）代表睁大的眼睛，右上角的图形（┐）是一个弯腰向下看的人，下面的（ㅍ）代表的是一个容器，容器上边的一横（一）表示装满了水。我们知道原始社会人们用水作镜子。这个字的本义就是"在水里照自己"。现在这个字的意思是"仔细地看或检查"。

　　An ideogram. In metal language, it was written as "盥". The sign on the upper left, "ϵ", signifies a wide-open eye, "┐" on the upper right a person bent low and looking downward, "ㅍ" in the lower half represents a vessel, and the horizontal line "一" above it indicates that it is filled to the brim with water. We now know that the primitive people used water as their mirror. The original meaning of this character then was looking down into the water to examine oneself. Now it means "to look at other people closely or to scrutinise".

【部首】Radical　　皿(vessel)

【同部首字】Characters under the radical
　　盆(basin)，益(benefit)，盐(salt)

【词语】Words and phrases

监察	jiānchá	supervise; control
监犯	jiānfàn	prisoner; convict
监护	jiānhù	guardianship

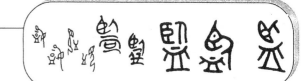

监考	jiānkǎo	invigilate
监牢	jiānláo	prison; jail
监票	jiānpiào	scrutinise balloting
监听	jiāntīng	monitor
监视	jiānshì	keep watch on; keep a lookout over

监察制度

　　jiān chá zhì dù

　　　　supervisory system

监督劳动

　　jiān dū láo dòng

　　　　do penal labour under surveillance

监守自盗

　　jiān shǒu zì dào

　　　　steal what is entrusted to one's care; embezzle

【例句】Example

　　有一位警察在房外监视。

　　　　yǒu yí wèi jǐng chá zài fáng wài jiān shì

　　　　　　There is a policeman watching outside the house.

jiāng

(border; boundary)

ㄱ	ㄢ	弓	弜	弲	彁	彁	彁	弱	弱	弱	疆	疆	疆	疆	疆	疆	疆

　　这个象形字由三部分组成："弓"、"土"和"畺"。"土"是"土地"，"弓"是古时丈量土地用的工具，"畺"用三条横线把两块田地分开。所以这个字的含义就是"边界、界限"。

A pictogram consisting of three parts: 弓, 土 and 畺. 土 is earth or land, 弓 is an instrument to measure the land, and 畺 is composed of three horizontal lines separating the two farmland symbols. Hence the meaning "border or boundary".

【部首】 Radical　　弓(bow)

【同部首字】 Characters under the radical
　　弱(weak), 弹(bounce), 弯(curved)

【词语】 Words and phrases

疆场	jiāngchǎng	battlefield
疆界	jiāngjiè	boundary; border
疆土	jiāngtǔ	territory
疆域	jiāngyù	territory; domain

驰骋疆场

chí chěng jiāng chǎng

　　　demonstrate one's bravery on battlefield

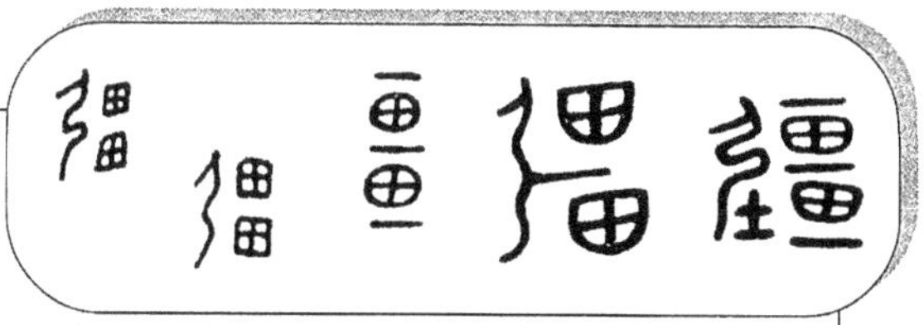

驻守边疆

zhù shǒu biān jiāng

stationed on the frontier

【例句】Example

保卫国家疆土完整，是军人的神圣职责。

bǎo wèi guó jiā jiāng tǔ wán zhěng, shì jūn rén de shénshèng zhí zé

It is the sacred duty of a soldier to safeguard the nation's territorial integrity.

jiāo

(proud; arrogant)

フ	马	马	马´	马二	马二	马二	骄	骄

　　这个象形字的左边是一匹马，右边是一个动词，表示"举高"。这个字的本义是"昂首的马"，或"不驯服的马"，后引申为"傲慢"。

Pictogram. The left part is a horse while the right is a verb meaning to lift high. The original meaning of this character was a horse raising its head high or an untamed horse. From that it was extended to mean being arrogant.

【部首】 Radical　　马(horse)

【同部首字】 Characters under the radical
　　驯(tame)，驰(gallop)，驱(drive)

【词语】 Words and phrases

骄傲	jiāo'ào	arrogant; conceited
骄横	jiāohéng	arrogant and imperious; overbearing
骄矜	jiāojīn	self-important; proud; haughty
骄气	jiāoqi	overbearing airs; arrogance
骄纵	jiāozòng	arrogant and wilful

骄傲自大

    jiāo ào zì dà

        swollen with pride; conceited and arrogant

骄兵必败

    jiāo bīng bì bài

        An army puffed up with pride is bound to lose.

骄阳似火

    jiāo yáng sì huǒ

        scorching sun

骄奢淫逸

    jiāo shē yín yì

        lordly, luxury-loving and wallowing in luxury and pleasure

胜不骄，败不馁

    shèng bù jiāo, bài bù něi

        not be dizzy with success, nor discouraged by failure

【例句】 Example

    她为人谦逊，毫无骄矜之态。

        tā wéi rén qiān xùn, háo wú jiāo jīn zhī tài

           She is modest, and never puts on airs.

解

jiě

(separate; dissect)

| ノ | ⺈ | ⺈ | 介 | 角 | 角 | 角 | 角⁄ | 解 | 解 | 解 | 解 | 解 |

　　由"角"、"牛"和"刀"三部分组成的"解"字，有"用一把刀将牛角切下"的含义，亦即"解剖"和"分切"的意思。

An ideogram composed of 角 (horn), 牛(ox) and 刀 (knife). To cut off the horn of an ox with a knife is to dissect, cut apart or separate.

【部首】 Radical　　角(horn)

【同部首字】 Characters under the radical
　　触(touch)

【词语】 Words and phrases

解馋	jiěchán	satisfy a craving for good food
解答	jiědá	answer; explain
解恨	jiěhèn	vent one's hatred; have one's hatred slaked
解决	jiějué	solve; resolve; settle
解渴	jiěkě	quench one's thirst
解释	jiěshì	explain; expound; interpret
解说	jiěshuō	explain orally; comment
解脱	jiětuō	free (or extricate) oneself

解除婚约

 jiě chú hūn yuē

  renounce an engagement

解放思想

 jiě fàng sī xiǎng

  emancipate the mind; free oneself from old ideas

解决争端

 jiě jué zhēng duān

  settle a dispute

解铃系铃

 jiě líng jì líng

  let him who tied the bell on the tiger take it off

   i.e., Whoever started the trouble should end it.

解囊相助

 jiě náng xiāng zhù

  help sb. generously with money

【例句】Example

 这西瓜真解渴。

  zhè xī guā zhēn jiě kě

   This watermelon really quenches your thrist.

jìn

(clean up;exhaust;to the utmost)

从甲骨文上，我们可以看出，这个字最初是由三部分组成的（ ）。底部的（ ）是一个容器，顶部的（ ）是一只手，中间是一个刷子（ ）。这个字的本义就是"手拿刷子清扫容器"。

From oracle bones,we find the origin of this character which consists of three parts " ". At the bottom is a vessel " ", on top is a hand " ", and in the middle, a brush " ". Holding a brush to clean a vessel, that is the original meaning of this pictogram.

【部首】 Radical　　尸(corpse)

【同部首字】 Characters under the radical
　　尺(ruler)，层(layer)，昼(daytime)

【词语】 Words and phrases

尽力	jìnlì	do all one can; try one's best
尽量	jìnliàng	to the full; try one's best
尽情	jìnqíng	to one's heart's content; as much as one likes
尽是	jìnshì	full of; all; without exception
尽头	jìntóu	end
尽兴	jìnxìng	to one's heart's content; enjoy oneself to the full
尽义务	jìnyìwù	do one's duty; fulfil one's obligation

尽职　　　　　jìnzhí　　　　fulfil one's duty

尽人皆知

　　jìn rén jiē zhī

　　　　be known to all; be common knowledge

尽情欢呼

　　jìn qíng huān hū

　　　　cheer heartily

尽善尽美

　　jìn shàn jìn měi

　　　　the acme of perfection; perfect

尽收眼底

　　jìn shōu yǎn dǐ

　　　　have a panoramic view

尽心竭力

　　jìn xīn jié lì

　　　　(do sth.) with all one's heart and all one's might

一言难尽

　　yì yán nán jìn

　　　　It can't be expressed in a few words.

【例句】 Example

　　他工作一向很尽职。

　　　　tā gōng zuò yí xiàng hěn jìn zhí

　　　　　　He has always been a conscientious worker.

jǐng

(a well)

一	二	丰	井

古时人们用的是井水，从图形（丼）可猜到，它是指地下有一个大洞，中间的小圆点便是井眼，旁边是井栏。在现今一些比较落后的村镇里，还可以找到"井"的足迹。

In metal language, this pictogram was written as "丼", indicting a big hole on the ground with boards placed around it forming a square. The dot in the middle represents the water inside.

【部首】Radical　　二(two)

【同部首字】Characters under the radical
亚(second)，互(mutual)，些(some)

【词语】Words and phrases

井壁	jǐngbì	wall of a well
井场	jǐngchǎng	well site
井底	jǐngdǐ	the bottom of a well
井架	jǐngjià	derrick
井口	jǐngkǒu	the mouth of a well; pithead; wellhead
井然	jǐngrán	orderly; neat and tidy; shipshape, methodical

井底之蛙

    jǐng dǐ zhī wā

        i.e., a person with a very limited outlook

井井有条

    jǐng jǐng yǒu tiáo

        in perfect order; shipshape; methodical

秩序井然

    zhì xù jǐng rán

        in good order

井水不犯河水

    jǐng shuǐ bú fàn hé shuǐ

        Well water does not intrude into river water.

           i.e., I'll mind my own business, you mind yours.

【例句】 Example

    中国有句俗话叫做：吃水不忘挖井人。

    zhōng guó yǒu jù sú huà jiào zuò: chī shuǐ bú wàng wā jǐng rén

        We Chinese have a saying: "When you drink the water, remember those who dug the well."

居

jū

(reside; residence)

| ㇀ | ㇆ | 尸 | 尸 | 居 | 居 | 居 | 居 |

　　古字中的"居"字，上面那部分画得像人的半边屁股（尸），这半边屁股要是在某个地方逗留了一段很长的时间（古），那便是人要定居下来的地方了。

In ancient times, "尸", the upper part of this character, referred to a person's buttock while 古, the lower part, meant staying put. To have one's buttock stay put in a place for an extended period is to reside.

【部首】 Radical　　　尸(corpse)

【同部首字】 Characters under the radical
　　屈(bend)，尾(tail)，局(part)

【词语】 Words and phrases

居多	jūduō	be in the majority
居功	jūgōng	claim credit for oneself
居留	jūliú	reside
居民	jūmín	resident; inhabitant
居然	jūrán	unexpectedly; to one's surprise
居士	jūshì	lay Buddhist
居住	jūzhù	live; reside; dwell

居高临下

    jū gāo lín xià

        occupy a commanding position (or height)

居功自傲

    jū gōng zì ào

        claim credit for oneself and become arrogant

居间调停

    jū jiān tiáo tíng

        mediate between two parties; act as mediator

居心不良

    jū xīn bù liáng

        harbour evil intentions

居中斡旋

    jū zhōng wò xuán

        mediate between disputants; be placed in the middle

居安思危

    jū ān sī wēi

        be prepared for danger in times of peace; be vigilant in peace time

【例句】Example

你怎么居然相信这种谣言。

    nǐ zěn me jū rán xiāng xìn zhè zhǒng yáo yán

        How could you believe such a rumour?

jūn

(ruler; sovereign)

乛	彐	彐	尹	尹	君	君

　　手拿权杖（月）再加上一个口（ㄩ），就是指"君"（月）。通常手拿权杖并发号施令的人就是一个地方的统治者，亦即"君主"、"国王"了。不过，后来也用来称谓对方；另外，品行好的人也称为"君子"。

In metal language, it was written as "月". The top part, "月" represents a hand holding a power stick and the lower part "ㄩ" a mouth. He who holds a power stick and orders people around is obviously a ruler. Later on, the character evolved to mean a sovereign.

【部首】 Radical 　　　口(mouth)

【同部首字】 Characters under the radical
　　右(right)，吃(eat)，呆(stay)

【词语】 Words and phrases

君权	jūnquán	monarchical power
君主	jūnzhǔ	monarch; sovereign
君子	jūnzǐ	a man of noble character; gentleman
诸君	zhūjūn	friends; gentlemen; ladies and gentlemen (a way of addressing a group)

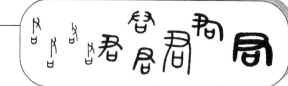

正人君子

> zhèng rén jūn zǐ

>> a man of moral integrity

君主立宪

> jūn zhǔ lì xiàn

>> constitutional monarchy

君主专制

> jūn zhǔ zhuān zhì

>> autocratic monarchy; absolute monarchy

君子成人之美

> jūn zǐ chéng rén zhī měi

>> A gentleman is always ready to help others attain their aims.

以小人之心，度君子之腹

> yǐ xiǎo rén zhī xīn, dù jūn zǐ zhī fù.

>> gauge the heart of a gentleman with one's own mean measure

【例句】Example

> 来访者乃君主本人。

>> lái fǎng zhě nǎi jūn zhǔ běn rén

>>> The visitor was none other than the monarch himself.

军

jūn

(troop; army)

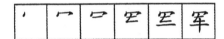

以前军人打仗时坐兵车，兵车的另一作用是作防护墙来保卫军队的阵营，所以从（）中可看到"车"是给（Ｏ）包围着，后来又多了"军队"的意思。

In ancient times, chariots were the vehicle used by warriors when they fought a battle. The chariots were also used as ramparts to protect the bivouac when troops on the march stopped overnight to rest. Hence the character "軍", which shows the character 车 being encircled. The "Ｏ" sign later evolved into "冖", and the character came to mean the army itself.

【部首】Radical　　　冖(cover)

【同部首字】Characters under the radical
　　写(write)，冠(champion)

【词语】Words and phrases

军备	jūnbèi	armament; arms
军方	jūnfāng	the military
军官	jūnguān	officer
军火	jūnhuǒ	munitions; arms and ammunition
军医	jūnyī	medical officer; military surgeon
军营	jūnyíng	military camp; barracks

| 军职 | jūnzhí | official post in the army; military appointment |
| 军装 | jūnzhuāng | military (or army) uniform; uniform |

军备竞赛

jūn bèi jìng sài

armament (or arms) race

军法审判

jūn fǎ shěn pàn

court-martial

军阀战争

jūn fá zhàn zhēng

war among warlords

军事训练

jūn shì xùn liàn

military training

军衔制度

jūn xián zhì dù

system of military ranks

军心大振

jūn xīn dà zhèn

The morale of the troops has been greatly raised.

【例句】Example

他的军龄比我长。

tā de jūn líng bǐ wǒ cháng

He has served in the army longer than I have.

寇

kòu

(bandit; intruder)

丶 丶 宀 宀 宀 宀 宀 完 完 完 寇 寇

在金文中，这个会意字显示出它的本义。它的上半部（宀）是一个房屋，（彡）是一个伸出头的人，（攴）是握着武器的手。合起来就是"一个拿着武器的人悄悄溜进房屋"，也就是"入侵者、匪徒"。

In metal language, this ideogram "寇" reveals its meaning right away. Its upper part "宀" represents a house or a room, "彡" the shape of a man with a protruding head and "攴" his hand holding a weapon. The combination depicts a man with a weapon sneaking into a house. Hence an "intruder", or a "bandit".

【部首】 Radical　　宀(roof)

【同部首字】 Characters under the radical
　　宁(peace)，室(room)，客(guest)

【词语】 Words and phrases

寇仇	kòuchóu	enemy; foe
敌寇	díkòu	the (invading) enemy
海寇	hǎikòu	pirate
入寇	rùkòu	invade (a country)

胜者为王，败者为寇

shèng zhě wéi wáng, bài zhě wéi kòu

He who wins becomes the king; he who loses becomes the bandit; history is written by the winners.

寇准背靴

kòu zhǔn bēi xuē

"Kou Zhun Carries His Boots," name of a Peking Opera about a Song Dynasty prime minister

【例句】Example

他们勇敢地抵抗凶残的敌寇。

tā mén yǒng gǎn de dǐ kàng xiōng cán de dí kòu

They stood up to the cruel enemy.

lǐ

(ceremomy; etiquette; rites)

`	㇕	礻	礻	礼

　　这个字左边的"示"表示上供祭品。右边的（豐），也写作（豐），表示丰收，它的下部（豆）代表的是高脚盘，上部是祭品，这也正是这个字的本义。现在这个字的意思是礼仪、仪式的统称。

　　On the left is the character 示 which means praying or presenting offerings before an altar. On the right is the character "豐", which is another version of "豐", meaning abundant or sumptuous, its lower part "豆" representing a long-legged plate and the upper part "豐", the offerings. That was the original meaning. Now it has come to mean rituals or ceremony in general.

【部首】Radical　　　礻(indicate)

【同部首字】Characters under the radical
　　祝(bless)，福(good fortune)，社(society)

【词语】Words and phrases
礼拜	lǐbài	religious service
礼服	lǐfú	ceremonial robe; formal attire
礼花	lǐhuā	fireworks display
礼教	lǐjiào	the Confucian or feudal ethical code
礼貌	lǐmào	courtesy; politeness; manners

| 礼品 | lǐpǐn | gift; present |
| 礼物 | lǐwù | gift; present |

礼尚往来

lǐ shàng wǎng lái

courtesy demands reciprocity

彬彬有礼

bīn bīn yǒu lǐ

refined and courteous

社交礼节

shè jiāo lǐ jié

social etiquette

礼轻情意重

lǐ qīng qíng yì zhòng

The gift is trifling but the feeling is profound; it's nothing much, but it's the thought that counts.

【例句】 Example

这是礼节上所需要的。

zhè shì lǐ jié shàng suǒ xū yào de

This is required by protocol.

立

lì

(stand)

丶	亠	亠	亡	立

古时候，"立"是这样子的（𡗜），上面是一个手脚伸开的"人"（大），下面有一划，代表"地面"。一个站着的姿势，就是"立"

Pictogram. In metal language it was "𡗜". Its upper part "大"represents a person with arms and legs out-stretched. Beneath it a horizontal line, meaning the ground. Surely when a person is doing that, he or she is standing and not sitting.

【部首】Radical　　立(stand)

【同部首字】Characters under the radical
站(stand)，章(chapter)

【词语】Words and phrases

立案	lì'àn	register; put on record
立场	lìchǎng	position; standpoint
立功	lìgōng	render meritorious service; do a deed of merit; win honour; make contributions
立柜	lìguì	clothes closet; wardrobe; hanging cupboard
立即	lìjí	immediately; at once; promptly
立誓	lìshì	take an oath; vow
立体	lìtǐ	three-dimensional; stereoscopic

立足点　　　　lìzúdiǎn　　　　foothold; footing

立场坚定

　　lì chǎng jiān dìng

　　　　be steadfast in one's stand; take a firm stand

立见功效

　　lì jiàn gōng xiào

　　　　produce immediate results; feel the effect immediately

立候回音

　　lì hòu huí yīn

　　　　An immediate reply is requested.

立竿见影

　　lì gān jiàn yǐng

　　　　set up a pole and see its shadow

　　　　　　i.e., get instant results

立锥之地

　　lì zhuī zhī dì

　　　　a place to stick an awl

　　　　　　i.e., a tiny bit of land

立于不败之地

　　lì yú bú bài zhī dì

　　　　establish oneself in an unassailable position; remain invincible; be in
　　　　an impregnable position

【例句】Example

　　这幅画立意新颖。

　　　　zhè fú huà lì yì xīn yǐng

　　　　　　This painting shows an interesting new approach.

lì

(beauty; pairing)

一　厂　厅　厅　丽　丽　丽

象形字。古代金文中写成：（）。下半部分（鹿）是一头鹿，上半部分（丽）是它的两只长长的鹿角。两部分结合起来，引申为美丽或者和谐的意思。

Pictogram. In metal language it looks like this "". The lower part "" is a deer and the upper part "" its two large spreading horns. The combination means, by extension, beauty or forming company.

【部首】Radical　　一(horizontal line)

【同部首字】Characters under the radical
　　不(no)，天(sky)，来(come)

【词语】Words and phrases

丽人	lìrén	a beauty
佳丽	jiālì	beautiful women
美丽	měilì	beautiful
秀丽	xiùlì	pretty; graceful; elegant
壮丽	zhuànglì	magnificent; majestic

风和日丽

    fēng hé rì lì

        The wind is gentle and the sun radiant.

天生丽质

    tiān shēng lì zhì

        natural beauty

山河壮丽

    shān hé zhuàng lì

        a country's majestic scenery; beauty of the landscape

无所附丽

    wú suǒ fù lì

        no one to depend on

丽人如云

    lì rén rú yún

        beauties are numerous like clouds

【例句】Example

    她既美丽又聪明。

        tā jì měi lì yòu cōng míng

            Her beauty equals her intelligence.

历

lì

(experience; history; calendar)

一 厂 万 历

历字（秝）被分为两部分：（秝）是声符，表示读音，（屮）是脚部。人们常说："读万卷书，不如行万里路"，到过世界各地旅游的人，见识都比较广博，"历"就是这个意思，它后来还多了"历史"这个意义。

The same character on oracle bones "秝" had two signs on top, it is the generic term for farm produce. The symbol at the bottom "屮" represents the foot. Someone who leaves his footprints on large tracts of land is certainly well travelled and experienced. By extension, the character also means "history", and "calendar".

【部首】 Radical　　厂(cliff)

【同部首字】 Characters under the radical
　　厅(hall)，压(press)，厌(dislike)

【词语】 Words and phrases

历程	lìchéng	course
历次	lìcì	all previous
历代	lìdài	successive dynasties
历年	lìnián	over the years
历任	lìrèn	have successively held the posts of
历史	lìshǐ	history

历数   lìshǔ   count one by one

历尽艰辛

    lì jìn jiān xīn

        experienced all kinds of hardship

历代名画

    lì dài míng huà

        famous paintings through the ages

历历在目

    lì lì zài mù

        come clearly into view, leap up vividly before the eyes

历史潮流

    lì shǐ cháo liú

        the tide of history; historical trend

【例句】 Example

    在历次比赛中她都取得了优异的成绩。

        zài lì cì bǐ sài zhōng tā dōu qǔ dé le yōu yì de chéng jì

            She has done well in all past contests.

两

liǎng

(a measurement unit; a pair)

一	厂	兀	丙	丙	两	两

　　将两个铲形（卅）的钱币放在一起的重量，就是古时的重量单位：两。直到现在，在市场买菜时，也常常是以"斤两"来计算的。因为是两个钱币，所以又有"二"和"再"的意思。

From the metal language version "卅", we can see that the original meaning of this ideogram was two persons side by side, i.e., a pair. This character was later used as a measurement unit. One *liang* equals one-tenth of a *jin*, which is half a kilo.

【部首】 Radical 　　一(horizontal line)

【同部首字】 Characters under the radical

　　右(right)，井(well)，画(painting)

【词语】 Words and phrases

两边	liǎngbiān	both sides; both directions; both places
两便	liǎngbiàn	be convenient to both; make things easy for both
两极	liǎngjí	the two poles of the earth; the two poles (of a magnet or an electric battery)
两面	liǎngmiàn	two sides; both sides; two aspects
两难	liǎngnán	face a difficult choice; be in a dilemma
两手	liǎngshǒu	dual tactics

| 两性 | liǎngxìng | both sexes |
| 两样 | liǎngyàng | different |

两败俱伤

liǎng bài jù shāng

both sides suffer (or lose); neither side gains

两面三刀

liǎng miàn sān dāo

double-dealing

两全其美

liǎng quán qí měi

satisfy both sides; satisfy rival claims

两厢情愿

liǎng xiāng qíng yuàn

both parties are willing

两袖清风

liǎng xiù qīng fēng

(of an official) have clean hands; remain uncorrupted

两面夹攻

liǎng miàn jiā gōng

make a pincer attack; be caught in cross fire; be caught in a pincer attack

两耳不闻窗外事

liǎng ěr bù wén chuāng wài shì

not care what is going on outside one's window

i.e., be oblivious of the outside world

【例句】 Example

这张纸两面都写满了字。

zhè zhāng zhǐ liǎng miàn dōu xiě mǎn le zì

This piece of paper is covered with writing on both sides.

mào

(emit; prop up)

丶 冂 冂 日 冃 冃 冐 冒 冒

这个字的古字，像一个带着帽的人，后来字义有了变化，渐渐多了"向外透出"、"往上升"的意思，如"冒烟"、"冒泡"；之后还有"不顾"、"不加小心"、"假托"等含义。现在"冒"和"帽"可是两个不同的字，使用时不要混淆。

Pictogram. The ancient version of this character "冐" looked like a person with a head cover, but with his or her eyes "ⵔ" exposed. So the headgear for children came to be called 冒 (for adults it was called 冠 guan). Later, as the character also took on the meaning of "emit" and "crop up", a 巾 was added to 帽 for hats in general.

【部首】 Radical   日(sun)

【同部首字】 Characters under the radical
    曾(once), 最(most), 量(measure)

【词语】 Words and phrases

冒充	màochōng	pretend to be (sb. or sth. else); pass sb. or sth. off as
冒犯	màofàn	offend; affront
冒火	màohuǒ	burn with anger; get angry; flare up
冒昧	màomèi	make bold; venture; take the liberty
冒牌	màopái	a counterfeit of a well-known trade mark; imitation
冒失	màoshi	rash; abrupt

冒险   màoxiǎn   take a risk;
                                       take chances

冒充内行

    mào chōng nèi háng

        pretend to be an expert; pose as an expert

冒犯禁令

    mào fàn jìn lìng

        violate a prohibition

冒昧陈辞

    mào mèi chén cí

        make bold to express my views; venture an opinion

冒天下之大不韪

    mào tiān xià zhī dà bù wěi

        defy world opinion; risk universal condemnation; fly in the face of the
        will of the people

【例句】 Example

    她就爱冒险。

        tā jiù ài mào xiǎn

            She likes to take risks.

měi

(beautiful; delicious)

| 丶 | 丷 | 丷 | 丷 | 羊 | 羊 | 羊 | 美 | 美 |

由 "羊" (羊) 和 "大" (大) 字组成的 "美" (美)，是说又肥又大的羊是最美味的，古人还真懂得 "吃" 呢！后来这个字又多了 "美丽" 的含义。

An ideogram consisting of 羊 and 大. In metal language, it was "美", with the upper part "羊" looking like a sheep, and the lower part "大" meaning big, indicating a big, fat sheep which tastes delicious. Later the character evolved to mean "delicious" or "beautiful".

【部首】 Radical 羊(sheep)

【同部首字】 Characters under the radical
羔(lamb)，羡(admire)，姜(ginger)

【词语】 Words and phrases

美称	měichēng	laudatory title; good name
美德	měidé	virtue; moral excellence
美感	měigǎn	aesthetic feeling; aesthetic perception; sense of beauty
美观	měiguān	pleasing to the eye; beautiful; artistic
美好	měihǎo	fine; happy; glorious
美梦	měimèng	fond dream
美妙	měimiào	beautiful; splendid; wonderful
美术	měishù	the fine arts; art

美满婚姻

    měi mǎn hūn yīn

        happy marriage; conjugal happiness

美其名曰

    měi qí míng yuē

        call it by the fine-sounding name of

美术设计

    měi shù shè jì

        artistic design

美味小吃

    měi wèi xiǎo chī

        dainty snacks

美不胜收

    měi bú shèng shōu

        so many beautiful things that one simply can't take them all in

美中不足

    měi zhōng bù zú

        a blemish in an otherwise perfect thing; a fly in the ointment

【例句】Example

    瞧他这美劲儿。

        qiáo tā zhè měi jìn er

            Look how pleased he is with himself.

名

míng

(name)

丿 勹 夕 夕 名 名

　　"名"（名）是由上下两部分组成的：（丿）是指晚上太黑暗，难以辨认出人的相貌，因此要张开口（凵）说出自己的名字来进行联络。

In metal language, this ideogram was written as "名". The upper part "丿" represents night, so dark one cannot distinguish the face of someone nearby. The mouth sign "凵" underneath implies that one has to ask who that person is. Together, they convey the idea of telling someone else one's own name or inquiring about the other's name.

【部首】 Radical　　　□(mouth)

【同部首字】 Characters under the radical
吊(hang)，呻(groan)，含(contain)

【词语】 Words and phrases

名词	míngcí	noun; substantive; term; phrase
名单	míngdān	name list
名贵	míngguì	famous and precious; rare
名家	míngjiā	the School of Logicians (in the Spring and Autumn and Warring States Periods, 770-221 B.C.); a person of academic or artistic distinction; famous expert; master
名将	míngjiàng	famous general; great soldier

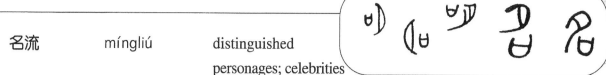

名流	míngliú	distinguished personages; celebrities
名声	míngshēng	reputation; repute; renown
名著	míngzhù	famous book; famous work

名山大川

　　míng shān dà chuān

　　　　famous mountains and great rivers

名正言顺

　　míng zhèng yán shùn

　　　　come within one's jurisdiction; be perfectly justifiable

名不副实

　　míng bú fù shí

　　　　the name falls short of the reality; be sth. more in name than in reality;

　　　　be unworthy of the name or title

名不虚传

　　míng bù xū chuán

　　　　have a well-deserved reputation; deserve the reputation one enjoys;

　　　　live up to one's reputation

名存实亡

　　míng cún shí wáng

　　　　cease to exist except in name; exist in name only

名副其实

　　míng fù qí shí

　　　　the name matches the reality; be sth. in reality as well as in name; be

　　　　worthy of the name

名列前茅

　　míng liè qián máo

　　　　be among the best of the successful candidates

【例句】Example

　　这种花的名字很特别。

　　　　zhè zhǒng huā de míng zì hěn tè bié

　　　　　　This flower has a peculiar name.

明

míng

(bright; clear)

丨	冂	冂	日	日刀	明	明	明

　　"明"（᷂）的左边是太阳（☉）或窗（⊕）；右边是月亮（᷂），阳光或月光从窗边射进屋里，便能带给人们光明了。在电灯还没有发明之前，人们便是靠这些自然光来照明的。

　　This pictogram was written as "᷂/᷂" in metal language. On the left is "☉" (the sun), or "⊕" (window), and on the right "᷂/᷂" (moon). Put together, they indicate that thanks to the sun and moon coming in through the window, the room is well lit. Hence "brightness".

【部首】 Radical　　　日(sun)

【同部首字】 Characters under the radical
　　昨(yesterday)，晚(late)，晒(shine)

【词语】 Words and phrases

明暗	míng'àn	light and shade
明白	míngbai	clear; obvious; plain; frank; unequivocal, explicit
明畅	míngchàng	lucid and smooth
明澈	míngchè	bright and limpid; transparent
明断	míngduàn	pass (fair) judgment
明朗	mínglǎng	bright and clear; obvious; forthright; bright and cheerful
明媚	míngmèi	bright and beautiful; radiant and enchanting
明星	míngxīng	star

明目张胆

    míng mù zhāng dǎn

        brazenly; flagrantly

明哲保身

    míng zhé bǎo shēn

        be worldly wise and play safe

明争暗斗

    míng zhēng àn dòu

        both open strife and veiled struggle

明辨是非

    míng biàn shì fēi

        make a clear distinction between right and wrong

明知故犯

    míng zhī gù fàn

        knowingly violate (discipline, etc.); deliberately break (a rule, etc.);

        do sth. one knows is wrong

明知故问

    míng zhī gù wèn

        ask a question while knowing the answer

明枪易躲，暗箭难防

    míng qiāng yì duǒ, àn jiàn nán fáng

        It is easy to dodge a spear shot in the open, but hard to guard against

        an arrow from a hidden corner.

【例句】Example

    他这样决定是明智的。

        tā zhè yàng jué dìng shì míng zhì de

            It was wise of him to make that decision.

mǔ

(mother)

"母" 字是指有儿女的妈妈。在字的两旁加上两点象征着一对特大的乳房（ ），这乳房就是用来给婴儿喂奶的。但这个字的位置后来改变了，但试试翻过来看，你还是能看见这个字最初的模样。

Originally, this pictogram was written as " ", indicating a woman with two big breasts, clearly distinguishing women who are married and have children from those who are unmarried or married but without children.

【部首】 Radical 　　毋(do not)

【同部首字】 Characters under the radical
每(per)，毒(poison)，毓(raise)

【词语】 Words and phrases

母爱	mǔ'ài	mother love; maternal love
母机	mǔjī	machine tool; mother aircraft; launching aircraft
母老虎	mǔlǎohǔ	tigress; vixen; shrew
母亲	mǔqīn	mother
母校	mǔxiào	one's old school; Alma Mater
母性	mǔxìng	maternal instinct
母语	mǔyǔ	mother tongue

母本植株

    mǔ běn zhí zhū

       maternal plant

母系亲属

    mǔ xì qīn shǔ

       maternal relatives

母系社会

    mǔ xì shè huì

       matriarchal society

失败是成功之母

    shī bài shì chéng gōng zhī mǔ

       Failure is the mother of success.

【例句】 Example

    她像母亲一样对待那些可怜的流浪儿童。

       tā xiàng mǔ qīn yí yàng duì dài nà xiē kě lián de liú làng ér tóng

       She was like a mother to the poor waifs.

尼

ní

(nun)

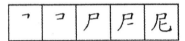

"尼" 和 "昵" 字相通，从古字（𣎆）可看到两个站得很亲密的人，正好表达了 "亲昵" 的意思。另外，住在佛寺里的女僧人叫 "尼姑"。

From the oracle bones "𣎆", we see two persons close to each other, in fact one with his back against the other's front. That was the original meaning of the character 尼 (also 昵). The expression 尼姑 or 比丘尼 is the transliteration of the Sanskrit word "Bhiksuni," which means a nun of the Buddhist faith.

【部首】 Radical   尸(corpse)

【同部首字】 Characters under the radical
　　尿(urine)，屁(fart)，展(exhibition)

【词语】 Words and phrases

尼庵	ní'ān	Buddhist nunnery
尼姑	nígū	Buddhist nun
尼古丁	nígǔdīng	nicotine
尼龙	nílóng	nylon
尼罗河	Níluóhé	the Nile

削发为尼

xuē fà wéi ní

becomes a nun

尼罗河惨案

ní luó hé cǎn àn

"Death on the Nile," a famous crime story by Agatha Christie

尼亚加拉瀑布

ní yà jiā lā pù bù

Niagara Falls

【例句】Example

他穿了一件尼龙料的衣服。

tā chuān le yí jiàn ní lóng liào de yī fú

He wore a dress made from nylon.

nián

(year)

象形字。甲骨文中"年"写成（ ）。下半部分（ ）是一个人；他的头上是麦子或水稻的谷穗（ ），（ ）代表丰收。在中国古代，农民每年收割一次。每当快到年底的时候，他们都要祭祖。因此，用一个头上有麦子或水稻谷穗的人"年"象征每年的祭祀活动。

Pictogram. In oracle bones, 年 was " ". The lower part is a man " "; on his head is an ear of wheat or rice " ", and " " represents harvest. In ancient China, farmers harvested one crop a year. As the year drew to a close, they would make offerings to their ancestors. That is why 年 is represented by a person with wheat or rice ears on his head as the symbol of the annual offerings.

【部首】 Radical　　丿 (left-falling)

【同部首字】 Characters under the radical
千(thousand)，瓜(melon)，午(noon)

【词语】 Words and phrases

年代	niándài	age; years; time; a decade of a century
年底	niándǐ	the end of the year
年糕	niángāo	New Year cake (made of glutinous rice flour)
年关	niánguān	the end of the year (formerly time for settling accounts)
年华	niánhuá	time; years

年货	niánhuò	special purchases for the Spring Festival
年景	niánjǐng	the year's harvest
年轮	niánlún	annual ring; growth ring

年富力强

  nián fù lì qiáng

    in the prime of life; in one's prime

年复一年

  nián fù yì nián

    year after year; year in year out; annually

年高德劭

  nián gāo dé shào

    of venerable age and eminent virtue; venerable

年深日久

  nián shēn rì jiǔ

    with the passage of time; as the years go by

虚度年华

  xū dù nián huá

    idle away one's time; waste one s life

【例句】 Example

  年代久了，石碑上的字迹已经模糊了。

    nián dài jiǔ le, shí bēi shàng de zì jì yǐ jīng mó hū le

      The inscriptions on the stone tablet have become blurred with the passage of time.

妻

qī

(wife)

一 ヲ ヨ ヨ 妻 妻 妻 妻

古时候这个字（妻）可真复杂！它的下半部分（妻）指的是一个女人正在用手（ヨ）把发簪插在头上（山），"女"、"手"、"发簪"三个象形部分就构成了"妻"的形象。古时候，女人结婚时要把头发梳成发髻。

In metal language, the ideogram "妻" looked much more complicated than now. The lower part "妻" represents a woman, who is using her hand "ヨ" to put hairpins "山"on her head. This was the kind of hairdo a woman wore during her wedding ceremony to indicate she was going to be the wife of a man.

【部首】Radical　　女(woman)

【同部首字】Characters under the radical
妹(younger sister)，姑(aunt)，姐(older sister)

【词语】Words and phrases

妻女	qīnǔ	the women of the family
妻子	qīzǐ	wife and children
妻子	qīzi	wife
人妻	rénqī	wife

妻儿老小

    qī ér lǎo xiǎo

        a married man's entire family

            i.e., parents, wife and children

妻离子散

    qī lí zǐ sàn

        breaking up or scattering of one's family

结发夫妻

    jié fà fū qī

        husband and wife by the first marriage

妻凭夫贵

    qī píng fū guì

        The wife's status grows with her husband's rise in position and power.

【例句】 Example

    她一定会成为一个好妻子。

        tā yí dìng huì chéng wéi yí gè hǎo qī zǐ

            She will make a good wife.

妾

qiè

(concubine)

丶	亠	亠	立	立	立	妾	妾

　　小篆中，这个字写成（妾）。上半部分（辛）代表行刑刀，意思是罪犯遭到惩罚。下半部分（女）代表一位女人。两部分组合起来表示一位女性战犯或者奴隶。这个会意字后来慢慢演变成了"男人的小妾"的意思。

　　In Little Zhuan, the character was written as " 妾 ". The upper part " 辛 " is the symbol of a torture knife, which implies that a criminal is under punishment. The lower part " 女 " represents a woman. Put together, they referred to a female prisoner of war or slave. Gradually, this ideogram evolved to mean a man's concubine.

【部首】 Radical　　女(woman)

【同部首字】 Characters under the radical
　　好(good)，奶(milk)，姓(surname)

【词语】 Words and phrases
　　纳妾　　　　nàqiè　　　　　take concubine
　　妻妾　　　　qīqiè　　　　　wife and concubine(s)

三妻六妾
　　sān qī liù qiè
　　　　three wives and six concubines (meaning many of them)

妻妾成群

qī qiè chéng qún

a flock of wives and concubines

【例句】Example

世界上仍有少数国家允许纳妾。

shì jiè shàng réng yǒu shǎo shù guó jiā yǔn xǔ nà qiè

There are in the world still a few countries which allow people to have concubines.

qìng

(festivities; celebration)

丶 一 广 广 庐 庆

从前"庆"写作（）。上边（ ）是鹿字的半边，中间（ ）是心，下边（ ）是脚。这个字要表达的意思是：一个人背着一只鹿献给他的亲人。由此得到"幸福"和"欢宴"的意思。

Originally, 庆 was written as "". The upper part "" was half of the character for deer, the middle part was "" for heart and the lower part "" for feet. What this character tries to convey is a man carrying a deer on his back to present to his beloved one. Hence the meaning "happiness" and "festivities".

【部首】Radical　　广(wide)

【同部首字】Characters under the radical
床(bed)，座(seat)，库(warehouse)

【词语】Words and phrases

庆典	qìngdiǎn	celebration; a ceremony to celebrate
庆功会	qìnggōng huì	victory meeting
庆贺	qìnghè	congratulate; celebrate
庆幸	qìngxìng	rejoice
庆祝	qìngzhù	celebrate

庆祝国庆

    qìng zhù guó qíng

        celebrate National Day

庆祝大会

    qìng zhù dà huì

        celebration meeting

盛大庆典

    shèng dà qìng diǎn

        grand celebrations

庆父不死，鲁难未已

    qìng fù bù sǐ, lǔ nàn wèi yǐ

        Until Qing Fu is done away with, the crisis in the state of Lu will not be over.

           i.e., There will always be trouble until he who stirs it up is removed.

【例句】Example

我庆幸自己死里逃生。

    wǒ qìng xìng zì jǐ sǐ lǐ táo shēng

        I congratulate myself on my narrow escape.

quán

(spring; fountain)

丿	亻	白	白	白	皀	身	泉	泉

古时的"泉"字是这样的（𤽄），其中（ᐟ）像一条河流；而（𦥑）是指环绕着河流的山，合起来就是指水从泉穴中流出，后来形成了河流。只看字形，相信你们都能猜到"泉"的意思。

In oracle bones, it was written as "𤽄". "ᐟ" was the symbol of a running stream and "𦥑" that of the surrounding mountains. This ideogram suggests water coming out from a cave or opening in the mountain. In other words, a spring or fountain.

【部首】 Radical　　水(water)

【同部首字】 Characters under the radical
永(forever)，求(ask)

【词语】 Words and phrases

矿泉	kuàngquán	mineral spring
喷泉	pēnquán	fountain
泉水	quánshuǐ	spring water; spring
泉眼	quányǎn	the mouth of a spring; spring
泉源	quányuán	fountainhead; springhead; wellspring; source
温泉	wēnquán	hot spring

泪如泉涌

    lèi rú quán yǒng

        tears well up in one's eyes

涌泉潺潺

    yǒng quán chán chán

        the bubbling of the spring

智慧的源泉

    zhì huì de yuán quán

        source of wisdom

力量的源泉

    lì liàng de yuán quán

        source of strength

【例句】Example

    这地方因温泉而出名。

        zhè dì fāng yīn wēn quán ér chū míng

           The place is famous for its hot springs.

rán

(right; like that; but)

ノ	ク	タ	夕	夕	外	然	然	然	然	然

　　小篆中，这个字写作（然）。（夕）在左上部表示肉，（犬）在右上部表示一只狗，下边的（火）表示火。这个字原来的意思是烤狗肉。现在的意义已经完全不同了。

In Little Zhuan, the character was written as "然". "夕" on the upper left represents flesh, "犬"on the upper right a dog and "火" down below a fire. The original meaning of this character was to barbecue dog's meat. Now it has taken on quite a different meaning.

【部首】 Radical　　灬(fire)

【同部首字】 Characters under the radical
　　热(hot)，黑(black)，燕(swallow)

【词语】 Words and phrases

忽然	hūrán	suddenly; all of a sudden
然而	rán'ér	yet; but; however
然后	ránhòu	then; after that; afterwards
然诺	ránnuò	promise; pledge
然则	ránzé	in that case; then
显然	xiǎnrán	obviously

不以为然

    bù yǐ wéi rán

        object to; not approve

大谬不然

    dà miù bù rán

        entirely wrong; absurd

巍然屹立

    wēi rán yì lì

        tower majestically

知其然，不知其所以然

    zhī qí rán, bù zhī qí suǒ yǐ rán

        know the hows but not the whys

【例句】 Example

    试验失败了多次，然而他们并不灰心。

        shì yàn shī bài le duō cì, rán ér tā mén bìng bù huī xīn

        Time after time they failed in the experiment, but they didn't lose heart.

rén

(humanity; benevolence)

ノ　イ　仁　仁

　　"仁"（仁）的左边是人（亻），右边的两条横线（二）指两个独立的个体。圣人孔子教我们要有仁心、仁爱，要相亲相爱，这样便能维持人与人之间友好的关系了。儒家学说中最推崇的就是"仁德"。

　　An ideogram with two components. On the left side is "亻", the radical for humans, and on the right side are two horizontal lines "二" implying two individuals. Together they refer to what governs human relationship, in other words, love and humanity. 仁 is one of the basic tenets of Confucianism.

【部首】 Radical 　　亻(person)

【同部首字】 Characters under the radical
　　　什(what)，伙(company)，依(obey; comply with)

【词语】 Words and phrases
仁爱	rén'ài	kind-heartedness
仁慈	réncí	benevolent; merciful; kind
仁兄	rénxiōng	my dear friend
仁政	rénzhèng	policy of benevolence; benevolent government

仁人志士

    rén rén zhì shì

        people with lofty ideals

仁义道德

    rén yì dào dé

        humanity, justice and virtue; virtue and morality

仁至义尽

    rén zhì yì jìn

        do everything called for by humanity and duty; do what is humanly
        possible to help show extreme forbearance

麻木不仁

    má mù bù rén

        insensitive; apathetic

仁者见仁，智者见智

    rén zhě jiàn rén, zhì zhě jiàn zhì

        the benevolent see benevolence and the wise see wisdom
            i.e., different people have different views

【例句】Example

    我们对这些人，真可谓到了仁至义尽。

        wǒ mén duì zhè xiē rén, zhēn kě wèi dào le rén zhì yì jìn

        We have really shown the utmost tolerance and patience towards
        these people.

荣

róng

(to flourish; glory; prosperity)

一	十	艹	艹	艹	艺	荭	荣	荣

你看"荣"（𣏌）像不像屋檐两边挂的饰物？"荣"是屋檐两边翘起的飞檐，看上去很宏伟的样子，因而有了"荣耀"和"繁荣"的意思。

In metal language, "𣏌" looked like two crossed flower stems or ears of wheat. It conveyed a flourishing picture. Hence the meaning "to flourish". The character has evolved to mean "glory" and "prosperity" too.

【部首】Radical   艹(grass)

【同部首字】Characters under the radical
　　劳(labour)，花(flower)，英(hero)

【词语】Words and phrases

荣归	róngguī	return in glory
荣获	rónghuò	have the honour to get or win
荣辱	róngrǔ	honour or disgrace
荣幸	róngxìng	be honoured
荣誉	róngyù	honour; credit; glory

春荣冬枯

    chūn róng dōng kū

        grow in spring and wither in winter

荣归故里

    róng guī gù lǐ

        return to one's native place with honour

荣华富贵

    róng huá fù guì

        glory; splendour, wealth and rank; high position and great wealth

荣辱与共

    róng rǔ yǔ gòng

        share weal and woe

荣誉称号

    róng yù chēng hào

        honorary titles

欣欣向荣

    xīn xīn xiàng róng

        flourishing; thriving; growing luxuriantly

【例句】 Example

    今天很荣幸能参加你们的晚会。

        jīn tiān hěn róng xìng néng cān jiā nǐ mén de wǎn huì

          It is a great honour to be with you at this evening party.

若

ruò

(as if; if)

一 十 艹 艹 芦 芹 若 若

我们要运用一下想像力才能猜到字的意思，"若"（ᵇ）字的中间部分原来是指一个长头发的人（ᵇ），两旁还有两只手（ᵗ ᵛ）在拨头发。这是"若"的本义，后来才解作"如果"、"不确定数目"，甚至有"你"的意思。

In oracle bones, this pictogram was written as "ᵇ" with the middle part "ᵇ" indicating a person with long hair, the symbols "ᵗ" and "ᵛ" on both sides representing her two hands raised to arrange her hair. That was the original meaning of this character. Now it means something quite different.

【部首】 Radical　　＋（grass）

【同部首字】 Characters under the radical
　　菜(vegetable)，范(model)，薄(thin; slight)

【词语】 Words and phrases

若虫	ruòchóng	nymph
若非	ruòfēi	if not; were it not for
若干	ruògān	certain number or amount; how many; how much
若是	ruòshì	if

若隐若现

    ruò yǐn ruò xiàn

        appear indistinctly

若有所失

    ruò yǒu suǒ shī

        feel as if something were missing; look distracted

若即若离

    ruò jí ruò lí

        be neither friendly nor aloof; maintain a lukewarm relationship; keep sb. at arm's length

若明若暗

    ruò míng ruò àn

        have an indistinct (or blurred) picture of; have a hazy (or vague) notion about

【例句】 Example

    若非亲身经历，岂知其中甘苦。

        ruò fēi qīn shēn jīng lì, qǐ zhī qí zhōng gān kǔ

           You cannot appreciate the difficulty except through personal experience.

shàn

(good; virtuous)

| 丶 | 丷 | 丷 | 丷 | 丷 | 羊 | 羊 | 羊 | 盖 | 盖 | 善 | 善 |

这个会意字原来是非常复杂的（𧮫）。上半部是一只"羊"，下边是两个代表说话的符号。"羊"通"祥"，意为吉祥。两个说话的符号说明一个以上的人在说话。中国有一个成语，叫"兼听则明"。这个字所描述的谈话肯定能带来好运，因为它让你向善。

The original form of this ideogram looked very complicated "𧮫". The top part is the character for sheep "羊", with two symbols for speaking "誩" below it. 羊 is also equivalent to 祥, which means auspicious. The combination of two speaking symbols indicate that there are more than one person speaking. There is a Chinese saying, "Listen to both sides and you will be enlightened." Such a conversation as described by the character will naturally bring good fortune because it makes you virtuous.

【部首】 Radical   口(mouth)

【同部首字】 Characters under the radical
　　喜(happiness)，售(sell)，唱(sing)

【词语】 Words and phrases
善本	shànběn	reliable text; good edition
善处	shànchǔ	deal discreetly with; conduct oneself well
善后	shànhòu	deal with problems arising from an accident, etc.
善良	shànliáng	good and honest; kind-hearted

善心	shànxīn	mercy; benevolence
善意	shànyì	goodwill; good intentions
善于	shànyú	be good at; be adept in
善终	shànzhōng	die a natural dealth; die in one's bed

善罢甘休

shàn bà gān xiū

leave the matter at that; let it go at that

善破善立

shàn pò shàn lì

be good at destroying the old and establishing the new

善始善终

shàn shǐ shàn zhōng

start well and end well; do well from start to finish; see sth. through

改恶从善

gǎi è cóng shàn

give up evil and return to good; mend one's way

心怀不善

xīn huái bú shàn

harbour ill intent

善有善报，恶有恶报

shàn yǒu shàn bào, è yǒu è bào

Good will be rewarded with good, and evil with evil.

【例句】Example

他是个很善良的人。

tā shì gè hěn shàn liáng de rén

He's a very good fellow.

圣

shèng

(sage; wise man)

| ㄱ | 又 | 圣 | 圣 | 圣 |

象形字，由三部分组成。(耳) 指耳朵，(口) 指嘴巴，(圣) 指国王。意即，能够听清并且明白谈话者话意的人有当国王的潜力。这样的人是圣人。这个意思和柏拉图的哲人王意义比较接近。

A pictogram with three components. 耳 is the ear, 口 is the mouth, 圣 the king. He who is able to listen and get the full implications of what the speaker is trying to say has the potential of being a king. That man is a sage. Compare this idea with Plato's philosopher king.

【部首】 Radical   土(earth)

【同部首字】 Characters under the radical
去(go)，坚(solid)，坏(bad)

【词语】 Words and phrases

圣餐	shèngcān	Holy Communion
圣诞	shèngdàn	the birthday of Jesus Christ; Christmas
圣地	shèngdì	the Holy Land (or City); sacred place of the Chinese revolution
圣洁	shèngjié	holy and pure
圣经	Shèngjīng	the Holy Bible; the Bible: Holy Writ
圣母	shèngmǔ	a female deity; goddess; the (Blessed) Virgin Mary; Madonna
圣贤	shèngxián	sages and men of virtue

圣旨　　　　　shèngzhǐ　　　　imperial edict

神圣领土

shén shèng lǐng tǔ

sacred territory

圣诞老人

shèng dàn lǎo rén

Santa Claus

古语云：人非圣贤，孰能无过

Gǔ yǔ yún: rén fēi shèng xián, shú néng wú guò

As the old saying goes, "Men are not saints, how can they be free from faults?"

【例句】Example

只有圣人才能容忍她的那几个孩子。

zhǐ yǒu shèng rén cái néng róng rěn tā de nà jǐ gè hái zǐ

You would need to be a saint to put up with her children.

十

shí

(ten)

一	十

　　甲骨文里，直立的（ **▮** ）就是"十"。"十"是十进制数字的最后一个数字，后来数字不断增加，这个字又多了一横，变成了（ **✦** ），让"十"之后的数字可以继续发展。

In oracle bones, a vertical line " **▮** " denotes ten. But as numbers kept on increasing in daily life, ten became a cross, i.e., a short horizontal line has been added across the vertical line as evident in metal language " **✦** ". This enabled the numbering to go beyond ten.

【部首】Radical　　十(ten)

【同部首字】Characters under the radical
　　卑(low)，千(thousand)，午(noon)

【词语】Words and phrases

十倍	shíbèi	ten times; tenfold
十成	shíchéng	100 percent
十分	shífēn	very; fully; utterly; extremely
十进制	shíjìnzhì	the decimal system
十六开	shíliùkāi	sixteen mo; 16 mo
十足	shízú	100 percent; out-and-out; sheer

十万火急

    shí wàn huǒ jí

        `posthaste; most urgent

十恶不赦

    shí è bú shè

        guilty of unpardonable evil; unpardonably wicked

十拿九稳

    shí ná jiǔ wěn

        90 percent sure; practically certain; in the bag

十全十美

    shí quán shí měi

        be perfect in every way; be the acme of perfection; leave nothing to be desired

十字街头

    shí zì jiē tóu

        crisscross street; busy city streets

【例句】 Example

    这样大的洪水真是十年九不遇。

        zhè yàng dà de hóng shuǐ zhēn shì shí nián jiǔ bú yù

            A flood of this sort is really unprecedented.

鼠

shǔ

(rat; mouse)

`	⺊	⺁	臼	臼	臼	臼	臼	臼	臼	鼠	鼠	鼠

　　"鼠"（🐭）画出了它的外貌：（Ⅶ）是牙齿，（🐾）是脚部，（ʔ）是长长的尾。老鼠常常偷吃人类的东西，又容易带来疾病，所以我们爱用"鼠辈"来形容令人讨厌的坏人。

In metal language, the rat pictogram was "🐭". Here you have "Ⅶ" to represent its developed teeth, "🐾" its fast-running feet and "ʔ" its long tail. Since hoary times, the rat has always been man's enemy. It is very much hated for the trouble it causes. In Chinese, all expressions associated with the rat have derogatory connotations. For example, 鼠辈 scoundrels; 鼠窜 scamper off like a rat; 鼠目寸光 see only what is under one's nose (the eyes of a rat).

【部首】 Radical　　　鼠(mouse)

【同部首字】 Characters under the radical
　　鼬(weasel)

【词语】 Words and phrases

鼠辈	shǔbèi	mean creatures; scoundrels
鼠疮	shǔchuāng	scrofula
鼠窜	shǔcuàn	scamper off like a rat; scurry away like frightened rats
鼠疫	shǔyì	the plague

鼠窜狼奔

    shǔ cuàn láng bēn

      run hither and thither like rats and wolves

鼠肚鸡肠

    shǔ dù jī cháng

      petty-minded, narrow-minded

鼠目寸光

    shǔ mù cùn guāng

      a mouse can see only an inch; see only what is under one's nose; be shortsighted

鼠窃狗偷

    shǔ qiè gǒu tōu

      filch like rats and snatch like dogs

        i.e., play petty tricks on the sly

【例句】 Example

  我们的猫很会捕鼠。

    wǒ mén de māo hěn huì bǔ shǔ

      Our cat catches mouses well.

shuì

(sleep; asleep)

| 丨 | 冂 | 冃 | 爿 | 目 | 目ˊ | 目˝ | 盯 | 盯 | 盰 | 睅 | 睡 | 睡 |

　　由"目"和"垂"两个字，组成了这个字：左边是眼睛，右边是垂下，当我们的眼皮垂下来的时候，是不是要去睡觉呢？

Pictophonetic character composed of 目 and 垂. On the left side is the eye symbol and on the right is a character meaning drop. When one's eyelid drops, he or she is most probably asleep.

【部首】Radical　　目(eye)

【同部首字】Characters under the radical
　　眠(sleep)，睁(open eyes)，睛(eyeball)

【词语】Words and phrases

睡觉	shuìjiào	sleep
睡莲	shuìlián	water lily
睡帽	shuìmào	nightcap
睡梦	shuìmèng	sleep; slumber
睡眠	shuìmián	sleep
睡醒	shuìxǐng	wake up
睡意	shuìyì	sleepiness; drowsiness

睡梦状态

    shuì mèng zhuàng tài

        dream state

睡眠障碍

    shuì mián zhàng ài

        sleep-disorder; somnipathy

早起早睡

    zǎo qǐ zǎo shuì

        early to bed and early to rise

睡眠不足

    shuì mián bù zú

        not have enough sleep

【例句】 Example

    马上上床，好好地睡一觉。

        mǎ shàng shàng chuáng, hǎo hǎo de shuì yí jiào

            Get straight into bed and have a good sleep.

sī

(private; selfish)

一　二　千　禾　禾　私　私

　　这个字的左边是"禾"，指禾稻；而右边是（厶），指用绳子把禾稻捆绑在一起拿回家去。"私"为私田的意思，后来引申至"个人的"、"自己的"意思。

The left side of this ideogram is the crop radical 禾 .The right side "厶" implies binding the crops into a bundle with a rope and taking it home. This conveyed the idea of ownership, something private.

【部首】Radical　　禾(standing grain)

【同部首字】Characters under the radical
　　秀(elegant)，秒(second)，称(weigh)

【词语】Words and phrases

私奔	sībēn	elopement
私娼	sīchāng	unlicensed prostitute
私仇	sīchóu	personal enmity (or grudge)
私愤	sīfèn	personal spite
私念	sīniàn	selfish motives (or ideas)
私事	sīshì	private (or personal) affairs
私通	sītōng	have a secret communication with

私有财产

    sī yǒu cái chǎn

        private property

窃窃私语

    qiè qiè sī yǔ

        talk in whispers

不谋私利

    bù móu sī lì

        seek no personal gain

私相授受

    sī xiāng shòu shòu

        privately give and privately accept; make an illicit transfer

私心杂念

    sī xīn zá niàn

        selfish ideas and personal considerations

不徇私情

    bù xún sī qíng

        not swayed by personal considerations

【例句】 Example

本阅览室参考书不得私自携出。

    běn yuè lǎn shì cān kǎo shū bù dé sī zì xié chū

        No reference books are to be taken out of the reading room without permission.

sūn

(grandson)

㇇	了	孑	孖	孙	孙

这个字在金文里写做（𦭞），左边的（𤕟）指儿子，右边的（𣎵）指一条绳上的两个扣。两部分连在一起，这个会意字表示儿子们的延续，也即孙子。

In metal language it was "𦭞", the left side "𤕟" being the son symbol and the right side "𣎵" two knots tied on a string. When the two parts are linked together, this ideogram implies a continuing line of sons and therefore grandsons.

【部首】Radical   子(son)

【同部首字】Characters under the radical
学(study)，孩(child)，孝(dutiful)

【词语】Words and phrases

孙女	sūnnǚ	granddaughter
孙媳妇	sūnxífu	grandson's wife; granddaughter-in-law
孙子	sūnzi	grandson
子孙	zǐsūn	posterity

子子孙孙
zǐ zǐ sūn sūn
    generation after generation of descendants

子孙后代

zǐ sūn hòu dài

coming generations; descendants

孝子贤孙

xiào zǐ xián sūn

worthy progeny; true son

孙子兵法

sūn zǐ bīng fǎ

Sun Zi's Art of War

【例句】 Example

她伤心地看着她死去的孙子的照片。

tā shāng xīn de kàn zhè tā sǐ qù de sūn zi de zhào piān

She looks sadly at a photo of her dead grandson.

tài

(greatest; excessively)

一	丆	大	太

　　不说不知，原来古时的"大"和"太"是同一个字，后来在"大"字上加多一点就成了"太"。"太"像一个男人骑着另一个男人（𠬠）的模样，二人的高度加起来自然让人想起"巨大"、"高大"的意思。

　　In ancient times, 大 and 太 were the same character. A horizontal line was later added to 大 to make 太. In the oracle bones, two men were put together to make the character "𠬠", pointing to the unusual height and thus conveying the sense of greatness. In Zhuan language, two horizontal lines were placed under 大 to stress the greatness.

【部首】Radical　　大(big)

【同部首字】Characters under the radical
　　央(center)，夷(safe)，奈(however, how)

【词语】Words and phrases

太后	tàihòu	mother of an emperor; empress dowager; queen mother
太监	tàijiān	(court) eunuch
太极拳	tàijíquán	taijiquan, a kind of traditional Chinese shadow boxing
太庙	tàimiào	the Imperial Ancestral Temple
太平	tàipíng	peace and tranquility
太平洋	Tàipíngyáng	the Pacific (Ocean)

太阳　　　　tàiyáng　　　the sun

太平盛事
　　tài píng shèng shì
　　　　times of peace and prosperity

太平天国
　　tài píng tiān guó
　　　　the Taiping Heavenly Kingdom (1851-1864), established by Hong
　　　　Xiuquan during the Taiping Revolution, the largest of peasant upris-
　　　　ings in China's history

太岁头上动土
　　tài suì tóu shàng dòng tǔ
　　　　provoke sb. far superior in power or strength

太公钓鱼，愿者上钩
　　tài gōng diào yú, yuàn zhě shàng gōu
　　　　like the fish rising to Jiang Tai Gong's hookless and baitless line
　　　　　　i.e., a willing victim letting himself be caught

【例句】Example
　　今天太阳很好。
　　　　jīn tiān tài yáng hěn hǎo
　　　　　　It's a lovely sunny day.

tān

(crave for; greedy)

丿	八	入	今	今	含	贪	贪

这个会意字由"今"和"贝"组成。下边的字代表钱和财产，上半部的（△）表示把东西藏在屋顶下的动作。因此"贪"指把某人的财产藏到屋顶下。后来它的意思变成了渴望或者贪图财富或者其它东西。

An ideogram composed of 今 and 贝. The latter represents money or property while the top part of "△" conveys the act of hiding something under the roof. 贪 therefore means hiding one's property under the roof. Later on it came to mean hankering after or greedy for wealth or other things.

【部首】 Radical   贝(shell)

【同部首字】 Characters under the radical
    贫(poor)，婴(baby)，购(buy)

【词语】 Words and phrases

贪婪	tānlán	avaricious; greedy; rapacious
贪恋	tānliàn	be reluctant to part with; hate to leave; cling to
贪图	tāntú	seek; hanker after; covet
贪污	tānwū	corruption; graft
贪心	tānxīn	greed; avarice; rapacity
贪赃	tānzāng	take bribes; practise graft

| 贪嘴 | tānzuǐ | greedy (for food); gluttonous |

贪得无厌

    tān dé wú yàn

        be insatiably avaricious

贪官污吏

    tān guān wū lì

        corrupt officials; venal official

贪生怕死

    tān shēng pà sǐ

        cravenly cling to life instead of braving death; care for nothing but saving one's skin; be mortally afraid of death

贪天之功

    tān tiān zhī gōng

        arrogate to oneself the merits of others; claim credit for other people's achievements

贪小失大

    tān xiǎo shī dà

        covet a little and lose a lot; seek small gains but incur big losses

贪赃枉法

    tān zāng wǎng fǎ

        take bribes and bend the law; pervert justice for a bribe

【例句】 Example

她贪图便宜在市场上买了几条裤子。

    tā tān tú pián yì zài shì chǎng shàng mǎi le jǐ tiáo kù zǐ

        She got some trousers on the cheap down at the market.

tián

(farmland)

　　甲骨文的"田"字（⊞）很有趣，看上去像很多小方格，其实是一块块排列着的田地。田是种庄稼的地方，它后来渐渐由小方格简化为现今常用的"田"字。

This pictogram was written like this "⊞" in oracle bones. It represented the ridges or ditches which separate the patches of farmland. Notice that the lines were not strictly regular, for that was what the farmland looked like in those days. By the time of metal language, the character had already become very close to its present form "⊕".

【部首】Radical　　田(farmland)

【同部首字】Characters under the radical
　　男(male)，思(think)，留(remain; leave)

【词语】Words and phrases

田地	tiándì	field; farmland; cropland; wretched situation; plight
田赋	tiánfù	feudal land tax
田埂	tiángěng	a low bank of earth between fields; ridge
田鸡	tiánjī	frog
田间	tiánjiān	field; farm
田径	tiánjìng	track and field
田园	tiányuán	fields and gardens; countryside

田庄　　　　tiánzhuāng　　　country estate

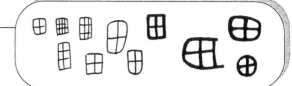

田间管理
　　tián jiān guǎn lǐ
　　　　field management

田径运动
　　tián jìng yùn dòng
　　　　track and field sport; athletics

田园风光
　　tián yuán fēng guāng
　　　　rural scenery

田园生活
　　tián yuán shēng huó
　　　　idyllic life

【例句】Example
　　你怎么落到这步田地?
　　　　nǐ zěn me luò dào zhè bù tián dì
　　　　　　How did you get into such a plight?

tù

(rabbit)

ノ	⺈	⺈	⺈	刍	乌	兔	兔

　　"兔"的象形字（🐰），突显了它的两只大耳朵，很可爱；在篆文中（🐇），则偏重在它的大尾巴上（🐇），两个写法都同样有趣。

　　In oracle bones, "🐰" bears the likeness of a rabbit, emphasizing its two large ears. The Zhuan script "🐇" on the other hand stresses its big tail "🐇".

【部首】Radical　　　⺈ (knife)

【同部首字】Characters under the radical
　　免(avoid)，危(danger)，色(colour)，负(bear)，争(contend)

【词语】Words and phrases

家兔	jiātù	rabbit
兔唇	tùchún	harelip
兔脱	tùtuō	run away like a hare; escape; flee
兔崽子	tùzǎizi	brat; bastard
兔子	tùzi	hare; rabbit
野兔	yětù	hare

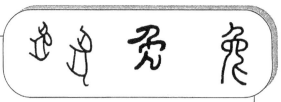

兔死狐悲

　　tù sǐ hú bēi

　　　　The fox mourns the death of the hare.

　　　　　　i.e., Like grieves for like.

兔死狗烹

　　tù sǐ gǒu pēng

　　　　The hounds are killed for food once all the hares are bagged.

　　　　　　i.e., Trusted aides are eliminated when they have outlived their usefulness.

兔子不吃窝边草

　　tù zǐ bù chī wō biān cǎo

　　　　A rabbit doesn't eat the grass near its own hole (so that it will be protected) .

　　　　　　i.e., A villain doesn't harm his nextdoor neighbours.

兔子尾巴长不了

　　tù zǐ wěi bā cháng bù liǎo

　　　　The tail of a rabbit can't be long.

　　　　　　i.e., won't last long

【例句】 Example

　　他坐着等待一只兔子从洞穴里跑出来。

　　　　tā zuò zhè děng dài yì zhī tù zǐ cóng dòng xuè lǐ pǎo chū lái

　　　　　　He sat watching for a rabbit to come out of the burrow.

蜕

tuì

(slough off)

| 丶 | 口 | 口 | 中 | 虫 | 虫 | 虫 | 虫 | 虫 | 虫 | 蚣 | 蚜 | 蜕 |

这个字的左边"虫"指虫子和动物，比如蝉，蛇。右边"兑"的意思是脱落、抛弃。两边结合起来指蝉和蛇蜕皮的事实。

The left side of this character is the insect and animal symbol 虫, such as 蝉(cicada), 蛇 (snake). The right side 兑 has the meaning of sloughing off, getting rid of. This combination refers to the fact that cicadas and snakes slough off their skin.

【部首】 Radical   虫(insect)

【同部首字】 Characters under the radical
　　蚁(ant)，虽(although)，蚤(flea)

【词语】 Words and phrases

蛇蜕	shétuì	snake slough
蜕变	tuìbiàn	change qualitatively; transform; transmute
蜕化	tuìhuà	slough off; exuviate
蜕皮	tuìpí	cast off (or shed) a skin; exuviate

感生蜕变

gǎn shēng tuì biàn

induced decay

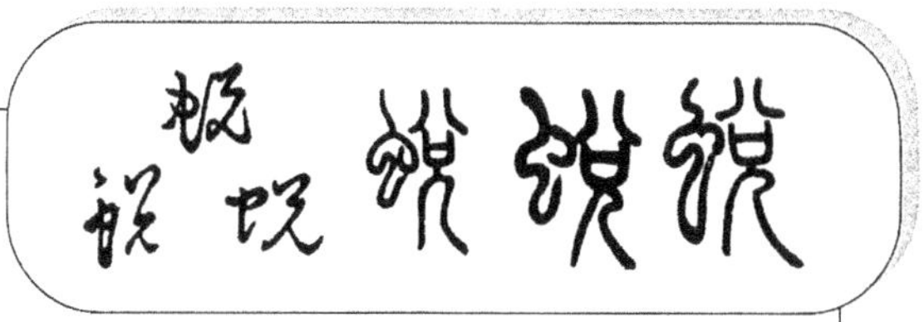

自发蜕变

zì fā tuì biàn

spontaneous decay

【例句】Example

我们在一块石头下发现了这条斑驳的蛇蜕。

wǒ mén zài yí kuài shí tóu xià fā xiàn le zhè tiáo bān bó de shé tuì

We found the mottled slough under a rock.

wàn

(ten thousand)

一	丁	万

这个字最早出现在甲骨文里，令人吃惊的是写成蝎（）。蝎子是一种可怕的动物，被它咬一下会很疼，甚至致命。金文里写成（），两只人手的符号（）加在蝎子的尾巴上，提醒读者，如果想抓住一只蝎子，应该首先抓住它的尾巴。后来这个意思转化了，一个数字达到万的时候，它就像蝎子一样可怕。您可以注意一下，全世界只有中国人和印度人用"万"作为计量单位。

The origin of this character may be found in oracle bones, surprisingly presented as a scorpion "". Now the scorpion is an awesome animal whose bites can cause extreme pain and even death. In metal language "", the sign of two human hands "" is added to the scorpion's tail, reminding the reader that when one tries to catch a scorpion, he should first get hold of its tail. The idea is transferred to mean when a number reaches ten thousand, it becomes as terrifying as the scorpion. Notice that throughout the world, only Chinese and Indians use ten thousand (lakh in India) as a counting unit.

【部首】 Radical 一(horizontal line)

【同部首字】 Characters under the radical
开(open)，有(have)，死(die)

【词语】 Words and phrases
万分　　　　wànfēn　　　　very much; extremely

万难	wànnán	all difficulties
万能	wànnéng	omnipotent;
		all-powerful; universal; all-purpose
万事	wànshì	all things; everything
万岁	wànsuì	long live
万物	wànwù	all things on earth
万象	wànxiàng	every phenomenon on earth; all manifestations of nature
万幸	wànxìng	very lucky (or fortunate); by sheer luck

万家灯火

    wàn jiā dēng huǒ

        a myriad twinkling lights (of a city)

万籁俱寂

    wàn lài jù jì

        all is quiet; silence reigns supreme

万马奔腾

    wàn mǎ bēn téng

        ten thousand horses galloping ahead

            i.e., going full steam ahead

万事亨通

    wàn shì hēng tōng

        Everything goes well.

万水千山

    wàn shuǐ qiān shān

        ten thousand crags and torrents

            i.e., the trials of a long journey

万无一失

    wàn wú yì shī

        no danger of anything going wrong; no risk at all; perfectly safe;

万紫千红

    wàn zǐ qiān hóng

        a riot (or blaze) of colour

【例句】 Example

    万一有人找我，就请他留个条。

        wàn yī yǒu rén zhǎo wǒ, jiù qǐng tā liú gè tiáo

            If by any chance somebody comes to see me, ask him to leave a

            message.

委

wěi

(submit; mild)

一	二	千	禾	禾	委	委	委

委（𦔻）的右边是垂下的稻穗（𣎧），左边是女人（𠨍），表示女子像禾穗那样弯曲下垂随风而动。从这个字的构造和来源，可以看到中国传统女性文雅、温顺和服从的性格特征。

In oracle bones, it was "𦔻", the right side "𣎧" being a drooping wheat ear, and the left "𠨍" a woman sign. The combination denotes gentleness and obedience traditionally associated with women.

【部首】 Radical　　女(woman)

【同部首字】 Characters under the radical
姨(aunt)，娱(amusement)，姿(posture)

【词语】 Words and phrases

委派	wěipài	appoint; delegate; designate
委任	wěirèn	appoint
委实	wěishí	really; indeed
委琐	wěisuǒ	petty; trifling; of wretched appearance
委托	wěituō	entrust; trust
委婉	wěiwǎn	mild and roundabout; tactful
委员	wěiyuán	committee member

委以重任

　　wěi yǐ zhòng rèn

　　　　entrust sb. with an important task

委靡不振

　　wěi mǐ bú zhèn

　　　　dispirited; in low spirits; dejected and apathetic

委曲求全

　　wěi qū qiú quán

　　　　compromise out of consideration for the general interest; stoop to
　　　　compromise

委系实情

　　wěi xì shí qíng

　　　　actually; certainly

委过于人

　　wěi guò yú rén

　　　　put the blame on sb. else

【例句】Example

　　对不起，委屈你了。

　　　　duì bù qǐ, wěi qū nǐ le

　　　　　　Sorry to have made you go through all this.

wù

(thing)

ノ	⺧	⺧	牛	牜	物	物	物

　　"物" 字本来的意思是身上长着不同毛色的牛，所以用牛作部首，由于牛的毛色很多，所以渐渐成为"事物繁杂"的意思。到了今天，"物"字多解做"事情"或"事物"。

　　Originally, 物 referred to an ox with hair of mixed colours. That's why it had an ox sign 牛 on the left. With time, this character has come to mean thing or matter. 万物, for example, means ten thousand things, or all things in the world.

【部首】 Radical　　牛(cattle)

【同部首字】 Characters under the radical
　　牧(herd)，牲(domestic animal)，牺(sacrifice)

【词语】 Words and phrases
物产	wùchǎn	products; produce
物价	wùjià	price
物件	wùjiàn	thing; article
物理	wùlǐ	innate laws of things; physics
物品	wùpǐn	article; goods
物色	wùsè	look for; seek out; choose
物证	wùzhèng	material evidence
物质	wùzhì	matter; substance; material

物归原主

　　wù guī yuán zhǔ

　　　　return sth. to its rightful owner

物换星移

　　wù huàn xīng yí

　　　　change of the seasons

物极必反

　　wù jí bì fǎn

　　　　things turn into their opposite when they reach the extreme

物尽其用

　　wù jìn qí yòng

　　　　make the best use of everything; let all things serve their proper
　　　　purpose

物以类聚

　　wù yǐ lèi jù

　　　　things of one kind come together; like attracts like; birds of a feather
　　　　flock together

【例句】 Example

　　你已把旅行用的物件收拾好了吗?

　　　　nǐ yǐ bǎ lǚ xíng yòng de wù jiàn shōu shí hǎo le ma

　　　　　　Have you packed your things for the journey?

xià

(down; under)

"下"字（⼀）由两部分组成：（⼀）代表土地；（−）代表"地下"。既然有上，就必定有下！

In oracle bones, this associative character looked like "⌒". The curve on top "⌒" signifies land, and the short horizontal line "˯" below it indicates underneath. Notice in "˯" (up) the short line is placed on top.

【部首】Radical　　⼀(horizontal line)

【同部首字】Characters under the radical
三(three)，丈(unit of length)，不(no)

【词语】Words and phrases

下摆	xiàbǎi	the lower hem of a gown, jacket or skirt; width of such a hem
下班	xiàbān	come or go off work; knock off
下策	xiàcè	a bad plan; an unwise decision; the worst thing to do
下场	xiàchǎng	go off stage; exit
下等	xiàděng	low-grade; inferior
下岗	xiàgǎng	be laid off
下贱	xiàjiàn	low; mean; degrading
下游	xiàyóu	lower reaches

正中下怀

    zhèng zhòng xià huái

        be exactly what one wants

下不为例

    xià bù wéi lì

        not to be taken as a precedent; not to be repeated

下车伊始

    xià chē yī shǐ

        the moment one alights from the official carriage

            i.e., the moment one takes up one's official post

下里巴人

    xià lǐ bā rén

        Song of the Rustic Poor (a folk song of the state of Chu); popular literature or art

下笔千言，离题万里

    xià bǐ qiān yán, lí tí wàn lǐ

        a thousand words from the pen in a stream, but ten thousand li away from the theme

            i.e., write quickly but stray from the theme

【例句】 Example

    她激动得说不下去。

        tā jī dòng de shuō bú xià qù

            She was so overcome with emotion that she couldn't go on.

xiān

(delicious)

⼀	⼁	⼂	⼃	⼄	⼅	⼆	⼇	⼈	⼉	⼊	⼋	鲜

　　甲骨文中，这个字是鱼和羊结合而成，或上下排列（𩼥），或左右排列（𩵋）。因为鱼和羊肉都非常好吃，两样结合后鲜美的意思更加清楚。

In oracle bones, this character is a combination of fish and sheep, either one on top of the other "𩼥" or sideways "𩵋". Since both fish and mutton taste delicious, the two together only serve to make the point clear to the reader.

【部首】Radical　　　鱼(fish)

【同部首字】Characters under the radical
　　　鲑(trout)，鲟(sturgeon)，鲤(carp)

【词语】Words and phrases

鲜红	xiānhóng	bright red; scarlet
鲜花	xiānhuā	fresh flowers; flowers
鲜美	xiānměi	delicious; tasty
鲜明	xiānmíng	(or colour) bright
鲜嫩	xiānnèn	fresh and tender
鲜血	xiānxuè	blood
鲜艳	xiānyàn	bright-coloured; gaily-coloured

鲜艳夺目

xiān yàn duó mù

dazzlingly beautiful; resplendent

色彩鲜明

sè cǎi xiān míng

in bright colours; bright-coloured; clear-cut; distinct

主题鲜明

zhǔ tí xiān míng

have a distinct theme

颜色鲜艳

yán sè xiān yàn

in gay colours

【例句】Example

这块布颜色太鲜。

zhè kuài bù yán sè tài xiān

This cloth is too bright.

祥

xiáng

(auspicious)

`	㇇	㇈	礻	礻	礻	祥	祥	祥	祥

　　以前人们祭祀时爱用羊来作祭品，祈求吉祥、吉利的兆头。"示"是指奉献或祈求，由"示"和"羊"合起来便成了"祥"。"恭喜发财"便是人们在新年时最爱说的吉祥话！

　　The left side of this pictograph 示 means to pray or give offerings, and the right 羊 the sheep. It was hoped that by offering a sheep as sacrifice to heaven, the prayer would get an auspicious omen.

【部首】 Radical　　示(indicate)

【同部首字】 Characters under the radical
　　社(society)，礼(courtesy)，祖(ancestor)

【词语】 Words and phrases

安祥	ānxiáng	composed; serene; unruffled
慈祥	cíxiáng	kindly
吉祥	jíxiáng	lucky; auspicious; propitious
祥瑞	xiángruì	auspicious sign; propitious omen

吉祥如意
　　jí xiáng rú yì
　　　　good fortune as one wishes

举止安祥

jǔ zhǐ ān xiáng

behave with composure

【例句】 Example

她是一个慈祥的老人。

tā shì yí gè cí xiáng de lǎo rén

She is a kindly old lady.

举止安祥

xíng

(shape)

| 一 | 二 | 干 | 开 | 开' | 形 | 形 |

古代人要测量一棵树的高度，就在它的近处竖起两根不同长度的棍子（开）。一个人躺在地上目测，使两棍的顶端与树顶在一条直线上，然后测量三者影子的长度（彡）。因此才有"形影"的说法。

To measure the length of a tree, the ancients placed two sticks "开" of varying length nearby. A person lying on the ground had the tops of the sticks and the tree in a straight line and then measured the length of the shadows "彡" they cast on the ground. That is the reason for the use of the expression 形影 (shape and shadow).

【部首】 Radical   彡 (feathery)

【同部首字】 Characters under the radical

彤(red)，参(join)，须(beard)

【词语】 Words and phrases

形成	xíngchéng	take shape; form
形迹	xíngjì	a person's movements and expression
形容	xíngróng	appearance; countenance
形式	xíngshì	form; shape
形态	xíngtài	form; shape; pattern
形象	xíngxiàng	image; form; figure

形状　　　　xíngzhuàng　　form; appearance; shape

形单影只
　　xíng dān yǐng zhī
　　　　a solitary form, a single shadow
　　　　　　i.e., extremely lonely; solitary

形式逻辑
　　xíng shì luó jí
　　　　formal logic

形象思维
　　xíng xiàng sī wéi
　　　　thinking in (terms of) images

形形色色
　　xíng xíng sè sè
　　　　of every hue; of all shades; of all forms; of every description

形影不离
　　xíng yǐng bù lí
　　　　inseparable as body and shadow; always together

形影相吊
　　xíng yǐng xiāng diào
　　　　body and shadow comforting each other
　　　　　　i.e., extremely lonely

【例句】 Example
　　这个艺术团已经形成了独特的风格。
　　　　zhè gè yì shù tuán yǐ jīng xíng chéng le dú tè de fēng gé
　　　　　　This performing art troupe has evolved a style of its own.

臭

xiù

(smell)

┌───┬───┬───┬───┬───┬───┬───┬───┬───┬───┐
│ ′ │ ⺅ │ 冂 │ 白 │ 自 │ 自 │ 臰 │ 臭 │ 臭 │ 臭 │
└───┴───┴───┴───┴───┴───┴───┴───┴───┴───┘

　　这是由"自"和"犬"两个字组合而成的字。在古代，前者的意思是鼻子，后者的意思是狗。狗的嗅觉非常灵敏，他们能闻到其它动物闻不到的气味。因此这个组合字的意思是闻。

An associative character composed of 自 and 犬. In ancient times, the former meant nose, while the latter dog. Dogs have a very sharp nose. They can smell what other animals can t. That s why the combination means smell.

【部首】 Radical　　自(self)

【同部首字】 Characters under the radical
　　息(rest)，鼻(nose)，臬(target)

【词语】 Words and phrases
乳臭	rǔxiù	smells of milk (meaning immature)
臭觉	xiùjué	sense of smell
臭神经	xiùshénjīng	scent
臭腺	xiùxiàn	scent gland

无色无臭

> wú sè wú xiù

>> colourless and odourless

无声无臭

> wú shēng wú xiù

>> noiseless and odourless

臭味相投

> xiù wèi xiāng tóu

>> share the same rotten tastes, habits; be two of a kind

乳臭未乾

> rǔ xiù wèi gān

>> still smell of one's mother's milk; be young and inexperienced; be wet behind the ears

【例句】Example

纯空气是无色无臭的。

> chún kōng qì shì wú sè wú xiù de

>> Pure air is colourless and odourless.

yī

(one)

一

这个字的结构很简单，它的来源不用说你也可猜得到：以前人们爱用食指代表数字"一"，因此就顺理成章造出了这个"一"字。它是十进制里第一个亦是最小的一个数字，可别小看它，在数字世界里不能没有它呀！

The ancients used the forefinger to express the number 一 one. It is the smallest whole number and the first number of the decimal system. 一 in the hoary past also meant I, the pronoun for the first person singular.

【部首】Radical   一(one)

【同部首字】Characters under the radical
    丙(third)，平(flat)，枣(date)

【词语】Words and phrases

一般	yìbān	same as; just like
一半	yíbàn	one half; half; in part
一边	yìbiān	one side
一次	yícì	once
一道	yídào	together; side by side; alongside
一等	yīděng	first-class; first-rate; top-grade
一贯	yíguàn	consistent; persistent; all along

一路　　　　　yílù　　　　　all the way; throughout the journey

一尘不染
　　yì chén bù rǎn
　　　　not soiled by a speck of dust; spotless
一筹莫展
　　yì chóu mò zhǎn
　　　　can find no way out; be at one's wits'end; be at the end of one's tether
一呼百应
　　yì hū bǎi yìng
　　　　Hundreds respond to a single call.
一箭双雕
　　yí jiàn shuāng diāo
　　　　shoot two hawks with one arrow; kill two birds with one stone
一刻千金
　　yí kè qiān jīn
　　　　Every minute is precious.
一脉相承
　　yí mài xiāng chéng
　　　　come down in one continuous line; can be traced to the same origin
一往情深
　　yì wǎng qíng shēn
　　　　be passionately devoted; be head over heels in love

【例句】Example
　　我只跟他见过一次面。
　　　　wǒ zhǐ gēn tā jiàn guò yí cì miàn
　　　　　　I've met him only once.

义

yì

(righteous; just)

丶	⁄	义

古代这个字（羛）上边是一只羊，下边是一只手和剑斧（戈）。意即这是一种有说服力的性格。

The ancient form of this character "羛" had a sheep sign 羊 on top and that of a hand 手 and a dagger-axe 戈 under it. This gives the idea of a forceful personality.

【部首】 Radical 丶 (dot)

【同部首字】 Characters under the radical
丹(red)，良(fine)，亲(relative)

【词语】 Words and phrases

义愤	yìfèn	righteous indignation; moral indignation
义举	yìjǔ	a magnanimous act undertaken for the public
义理	yìlǐ	argumentation (of a speech or essay)
义卖	yìmài	a sale of goods (usually at high prices) for charity or other worthy causes; charity bazaar
义气	yìqì	code of brotherhood; personal loyalty
义务	yìwù	duty; obligation
义演	yìyǎn	benefit performance

义不容辞

    yì bù róng cí

        be duty-bound; have an unshirkable duty

义愤填膺

    yì fèn tián yīng

        be filled with (righteous) indignation

义无反顾

    yì wú fǎn gù

        honour permits no turning back; be duty-bound not to turn back

义形于色

    yì xíng yú sè

        with indignation written on one's face

义正词严

    yì zhèng cí yán

        speak sternly out of a sense of justice; speak with the force of justice

【例句】Example

    我是来尽义务的。

        wǒ shì lái jìng yì wù de

           I've come to do voluntary service.

饮

yǐn

(drink)

最早，这个字的写法是（歆），后来逐渐演变为（䬷）。左边的（酓）是酒的古代写法，右边的（欠）指一个人张开大嘴喝酒。

Originally, it looked like "歆", from which it gradually evolved to "䬷". The sign on the left "酓" of this ancient character represents liquor, the sign on the right "欠" is the symbol of a person with his or her mouth open in order to swallow the liquor.

【部首】 Radical   饣 (eat)

【同部首字】 Characters under the radical
    饥(hungry)，饱(be full)，饭(meal)

【词语】 Words and phrases

冷饮	lěngyǐn	cold drinks
饮茶	yǐnchá	drink tea
饮料	yǐnliào	drink; beverage
饮食	yǐnshí	food and drink; diet
饮水器	yǐnshuǐqì	drinking bowl; drinker
饮用水	yǐnyòngshuǐ	drinking water; potable water

饮弹身亡

yǐn dàn shēn wáng

be killed by a bullet

饮恨而终

yǐn hèn ér zhōng

die with a grievance in one's heart

饮泣吞声

yǐn qì tūn shēng

swallow one's tears; weep silent tears

饮水思源

yǐn shuǐ sī yuán

when you drink water, think of its source

i.e., never forget where one's happiness comes from

饮鸩止渴

yǐn zhèn zhǐ kě

drink poison to quench thirst

i.e., seek temporary relief regardless of the consequences

【例句】 Example

他赚来的钱半数花在饮酒上。

tā zhuàn lái de qián bàn shù huā zài yǐn jiǔ shàng

He drinks half his earnings, spends it on alcoholic liquors.

yòu

(right)

一 ナ オ 右 右

古文里的"右"字有两个写法：(彐\)和（彐）。由"手"和"口"组成，表示用手和口来帮助工作。仔细看看，它像不像一个人正举起右手去拿东西？

From the metal language "彐\" and the Zhuan script "彐", one can detect that the right arm is moving to pick up something. It is the movement that is presented in the character.

【部首】Radical　　口(mouth)

【同部首字】Characters under the radical
台(tower)，兄(elder brother)，吵(quarrel)

【词语】Words and phrases

右边	yòubiān	the right (or right-hand) side; the right
右舵	yòuduò	right standard rudder; right rudder
右锋	yòufēng	right forward
右面	yòumiàn	the right (or right-hand) side
右手	yòushǒu	the right hand
右首	yòushǒu	the right-hand side; the right
右旋	yòuxuán	dextrorotation

右旋物质

  yòu xuán wù zhì

    dextrorotatory substance

右翼分子

  yòu yì fèn zǐ

    right-winger; member of the Right

无出其右

  wú chū qí yòu

    second to none

【例句】 Example

  她右首坐着一位老大娘。

    tā yòu shǒu zuò zhè yí wèi lǎo dà niáng

      An old woman was seated on his right.

yù

(prison)

丿 犭 犭 犭 犴 犾 犾 狱 狱

原始社会的时候没有监狱。抓住战犯后，用狗来看住他们。所以这个字的左右都是狗"犭，犬"。中间的"言"是表示说话的字，意思是让这些人和／或犯人坦白。后来，"狱"变成了"监狱"的意思。

In primitive society there was no prison. When prisoners of war were taken, dogs were used to keep watch over them. That is why on both sides of this character are the dog symbols "犭,犬". In the middle 言 is the character for speech, indicating that pows and/or criminals were expected to make confessions. Over time, 狱 has come to mean prison.

【部首】 Radical   犭 (dog)

【同部首字】 Characters under the radical
狐(fox)，猜(guess)，狗(dog)

【词语】 Words and phrases

断狱	duànyù	hear and pass judgment on a case
监狱	jiānyù	prison; jail
入狱	rùyù	be imprisoned
狱吏	yùlì	warder; prison officer; jailer
狱卒	yùzú	prison guard; turnkey
冤狱	yuānyù	an unjust charge; an unjust verdict

监狱看守

  jiān yù kān shǒu

    prison guard

投入监狱

  tóu rù jiān yù

    sent to prison; imprisoned

含冤入狱

  hán yuān rù yù

    imprisoned under a false charge

【例句】 Example

  她去监狱探望丈夫。

    tā qù jiān yù tàn wàng zhàng fū

      She went to the prison to visit her husband.

元

yuán

(beginning)

一	二	亍	元

这个字很有趣，把人的头部（●）加在人的身体（人）上，就是"元"（元）。它有"为首"的意思，后来有了"开始"的含义。猜一猜，"元首"是什么意思呢？

In both the oracle bones "元" and in metal script "元", a short line "●" was added to human sign "人", indicating it refers to a human's head. From this evolved the meaning of starting, beginning.

【部首】Radical　　儿(son)

【同部首字】Characters under the radical
　　　允(allow)，充(full)，兢(careful, cautious)

【词语】Words and phrases

元宝	yuánbǎo	a shoe-shaped gold or silver ingot used as money in feudal China
元旦	yuándàn	New Year's Day
元老	yuánlǎo	senior statesman; founding member (of a political organization, etc.)
元配	yuánpèi	first wife
元曲	yuánqǔ	a type of verse popular in the Yuan Dynasty (1271-1368), including *zaju* (杂剧) and *sanqu* (散曲), sometimes referring

		to *zaju* only
元首	yuánshǒu	head of a state
元凶	yuánxiōng	prime culprit; arch-criminal

元气旺盛
    yuán qì wàng shèng
        full of vitality

元素分析
    yuán sù fēn xī
        ultimate analysis

恢复元气
    huī fù yuán qì
        regain one's strength

开国元勋
    kāi guó yuán xūn
        founders of a state

【例句】Example
    元旦我想请一些朋友吃饭。
        yuán dàn wǒ xiǎng qǐng yì xiē péng yǒu chī fàn
        I'm going to entertain some of my friends on New Year's Day.

乐

yuè

(music)

一	匚	乕	乐	乐

　　从甲骨文（ᛘ）和活字（ᛘ）来看，这个象形字来源于一种树枝形状的乐器。一个木头把手（米）加上固定在上面的铃铛（ᛘ），这种乐器在祭祀祖先时候使用。后来演变成乐器奏出来的音乐。再后来变成了"高兴"的意思。

　　From the oracle bones "ᛘ" and the metal script "ᛘ",we could conclude that this pictograph originated from a tree-branch-shaped musical instrument. With a wooden handle "米" and bells "ᛘ"attached to it, this instrument was used during a sacrificial ceremony to ancestors. Later on it developed to mean music from the instrument. Still later it evolved to mean happiness.

【部首】Radical　　　一(left-falling)

【同部首字】Characters under the radical
　　生 (crude)，久(for a long time)，复(again, answer)

【词语】Words and phrases
乐池	yuèchí	orchestra pit
乐队	yuèduì	orchestra; band
乐府	yuèfǔ	an official conservatory in the Han Dynasty (206 BC-220AD) for collecting and composing folk songs and ballads
乐理	yuèlǐ	music theory

乐谱	yuèpǔ	music score
乐器	yuèqì	musical instrument
乐团	yuètuán	philharmonic orchestra
乐章	yuèzhāng	movement

乐队指挥

yuè duì zhǐ huī

conductor; bandmaster

交响乐队

jiāo xiǎng yuè duì

symphony (or philharmonic) orchestra

古典音乐

gǔ diǎn yīn yuè

classical music

管弦乐队

guǎn xián yuè duì

orchestra

【例句】Example

这孩子的音乐天分确实很高。

zhè hái zǐ de yīn yuè tiān fèn què shí hěn gāo

The kid is really highly musical.

孕

yùn

(pregnant)

在中国古文里，这个字写成（）。外面（）是一个人的身体，里面（）是个胎儿。

In ancient Chinese, this character looked like "". Outside "" is a human body and inside "" a foetus.

【部首】 Radical   子(child)

【同部首字】 Characters under the radical
孙(grandson)，学(study)，孩(child)

【词语】 Words and phrases

孕畜	yùnchù	pregnant domestic animal
孕妇	yùnfù	pregnant woman
孕期	yùnqī	pregnancy; gestation
孕穗	yùnsuì	booting
孕吐	yùntǔ	vomiting during pregnancy; morning sickness
孕育	yùnyù	be pregnant with

怀孕妇女

    huái yùn fù nǚ

        pregnant women

孕期反应

    yùn qī fǎn yìng

        pregnancy reaction

夫征不复，妇孕不育

    fū zhēng bú fù, fù yùn bú yù

        The wife cannot be pregnant with her husband away at the front.

【例句】Example

    他妻子怀孕已八个月了。

        tā qī zǐ huái yùn yǐ bā gè yuè le

        His wife is eight months pregnant.

zèng

(gift)

| 丨 | 冂 | 刀 | 贝 | 贝ˋ | 贝丶 | 贝丷 | 赠 | 赠 | 赠 | 赠 | 赠 | 赠 | 赠 | 赠 |

　　这个象形字（赠），左边是一个钱的符号（贝），右边是一种食品蒸屉的形状（曾）。把钱或者财物加在其他人的东西上，也就是赠送礼物的意思。

The left part of this ancient pictograph "赠" is the money symbol "贝", the right side has the shape of a food steamer "曾". To add one's own money or property to the vessels of other people is therefore to present a gift.

【部首】Radical　　　贝(shell)

【同部首字】Characters under the radical
　　败(fail)，财(wealth)，货(goods)

【词语】Words and phrases

赠答	zèngdá	present each other with gifts, poems, etc.
赠品	zèngpǐn	(complimentary) gift; giveaway
赠送	zèngsòng	give as a present; present as a gift
赠言	zèngyán	words of advice or encouragement given to a friend at parting
赠阅	zèngyuè	(of a book, periodical, etc.) given free by the publisher

赠送仪式

zèng sòng yí shì

presentation ceremony

临别赠言

lín bié zèng yán

parting words of advice or encouragement

相互赠送

xiāng hù zèng sòng

exchange gifts

接受赠品

jiē shòu zèng pǐn

accept a gift

【例句】 Example

他把他的藏书赠送给图书馆。

tā bǎ tā de cáng shū zèng sòng gěi tú shū guǎn

He gave his books to the library.

者

zhě

(that; which)

一 十 土 耂 耂 者 者 者

说起来你也想不到，"者"字本来的意思是"煮"东西。古时候，在金文中，可以看到这个"者"字（𤆥）下面有一口锅（𠙴）里装着一些食物（𤇾），里头还有两点（··），代表上升的水蒸气。不过到了现在，这个字的含义完全不同了，变成专指人、事、物等。

The original version of the pictograph is 煮 (to boil). We can detect from the metal script "𤆥" that there is a pot "𠙴" with some food "𤇾" inside, and the two dots " " on top represent the rising steam. Now it has come to indicate a class of persons or things.

【部首】Radical   日(sun)

【同部首字】Characters under the radical
　　旨(aim)，冒(emit)

【词语】Words and phrases

出版者	chūbǎnzhě	publisher
编者	biānzhě	editor; compiler
读者	dúzhě	reader
劳动者	láodòngzhě	labour; labourer
胜利者	shènglìzhě	victor
长者	zhǎngzhě	elder; senior
作者	zuòzhě	author

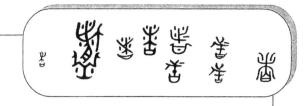

二者必居其一

  èr zhě bì jū qí yī

    It must be one or the other.

两者缺一不可

  liǎng zhě quē yī bù kě

    Neither is dispensable.

【例句】Example

  两个可能性中，后者比前者更可能。

    liǎng gè kě néng xìng zhōng, hòu zhě bǐ qián zhě gèng kě néng

      Of the two possibilities, the latter is more likely than the former.

zhèng

(straight; regular)

　　"正"字在甲骨文里是这样的（♀），上部（□）指城市，下部（Ψ）指脚印，象征着人们离开家乡去远征打仗，有"正向着那个方向"的意思。同时，它亦有正中、不偏不倚的意思。

This pictograph originally looked like "♀" in oracle bones. The top part "□" represents a city, the lower part "Ψ" footprints. When people walk towards cities other than their own, they are on armed expedition. That was the original meaning of this character. Now it means straight or regular.

【部首】 Radical　　止(stop)

【同部首字】 Characters under the radical
　　步(step)，歧(branch)

【词语】 Words and phrases

正常	zhèngcháng	normal; regular
正当	zhèngdāng	proper; appropriate; legitimate
正好	zhènghǎo	just in time; just right; just enough
正经	zhèngjing	decent; respectable; honest
正确	zhèngquè	correct; right; proper
正视	zhèngshì	face squarely; face up to; look squarely at

正义   zhèngyì   justice

正本清源

    zhèng běn qīng yuán

        radically reform; thoroughly overhaul

正襟危坐

    zhèng jīn wēi zuò

        straighten one's clothes and sit properly; be all seriousness

正人君子

    zhèng rén jūn zǐ

        a man of honour

正颜厉色

    zhèng yán lì sè

        look serious and severe; put on a stern countenance

正中下怀

    zhèng zhòng xià huái

        be just what one hopes for; fit in exactly with one's wishes

【例句】 Example

    现在咱们谈正事。

        xiàn zài zán mén tán zhèng shì

           Now let's talk business.

zhī

(branch)

一 十 才 木 木 术 枝 枝

　　"枝"是由古字"支"演变而来的，古时"支"字是由"十"和"又"所组成的。"十"代表树枝；而"又"代表手。行动有困难的人，有时要扶着树枝或用拐杖行走，后来人们再加上一个"木"字变成"枝"，就成了从树木主干分出来的"桠枝"。

支 is an associative character with two components 十 and 又. The former represents a tree branch, the latter a hand. When a man is hard at walking, he holds a tree branch or a stick to lean on. This character 支 used to be indistinguishable from the character 枝, which now means branch or twig.

【部首】Radical　　　木(tree)

【同部首字】Characters under the radical
　　松(pine)，枉(in vain)，板(board)

【词语】Words and phrases

枝杈	zhīchà	branch; twig
枝接	zhījiē	scion grafting
枝节	zhījié	branches and knots (minor matters)
枝蔓	zhīmàn	branches and tendrils (complicated and confused)
枝条	zhītiáo	branch; twig
枝叶	zhīyè	branches and leaves

枝子　　　　　zhīzi　　　　　branch; twig

横生枝节

　　héng shēng zhī jié

　　　　raise unexpected difficulties

一枝蜡烛

　　yì zhī là zhú

　　　　a candle

一枝梅花

　　yì zhī méi huā

　　　　a spray of plum blossoms

文字枝蔓，不得要领

　　wén zì zhī màn, bù dé yào lǐng

　　　　The writing is confused and the main points are not clear.

【例句】Example

　　那棵大樟树枝叶茂盛。

　　　　nà kē dà zhāng shù zhī yè mào shèng

　　　　　　The big camphor tree is a mass of branches and leaves.

字

zì

(word; Chinese character)

丶 丷 宀 宁 宁 字

（𡆥）的组成很有趣：上面是一间房屋（宀），里面有一个小童（子）。也许古人这样想：小孩子比较贪玩，不能集中精神学习，所以便安排他到房间里专心写字。

In ancient Chinese, this character looked like "𡆥". The top part "宀" is a house or room and inside "子" it a child. Children are easily distracted. To make them concentrate, teachers have to keep them in a classroom to study, first of all the Chinese characters.

【部首】Radical　　宀(roof)

【同部首字】Characters under the radical
安(safe)，完(finish)，宝(treasure)

【词语】Words and phrases

字典	zìdiǎn	dictionary
字画	zìhuà	calligraphy and painting
字迹	zìjì	handwriting
字谜	zìmí	a riddle about a character or word
字母	zìmǔ	letters of an alphabet
字体	zìtǐ	form of a written or printed character
字眼	zìyǎn	wording; diction
字样	zìyàng	model of written characters; printed or written words